BECOMING A MASTER AT SETTING BOUNDARIES

A 10-WEEK MASTER PLAN TO HELP YOU DISCOVER HOW TO SET LIMITS, EXPRESS YOUR NEEDS AND BUILD HEALTHY RELATIONSHIPS

ANDREI NEDELCU

© Copyright 2023 - All rights reserved.

The content contained within this book may not be reproduced, duplicated or transmitted without direct written permission from the author or the publisher.

Under no circumstances will any blame or legal responsibility be held against the publisher, or author, for any damages, reparation, or monetary loss due to the information contained within this book, either directly or indirectly.

Legal Notice:

This book is copyright protected. It is only for personal use. You cannot amend, distribute, sell, use, quote or paraphrase any part, or the content within this book, without the consent of the author or publisher.

Disclaimer Notice:

Please note the information contained within this document is for educational and entertainment purposes only. All effort has been executed to present accurate, up to date, reliable, complete information. No warranties of any kind are declared or implied. Readers acknowledge that the author is not engaged in the rendering of legal, financial, medical or professional advice. The content within this book has been derived from various sources. Please consult a licensed professional before attempting any techniques outlined in this book.

By reading this document, the reader agrees that under no circumstances is the author responsible for any losses, direct or indirect, that are incurred as a result of the use of the information contained within this document, including, but not limited to, errors, omissions, or inaccuracies.

TABLE OF CONTENTS

Introduction   7

Week 1 What Are Boundaries?   13
Week 2 What Really Happens When Our Boundaries Are Violated?   25
Week 3 What Really Happens If You Allow Your Boundaries to Take Care of You   39
Week 4 Master Your Personal Boundary Skills   53
Week 5 Boundaries and Friendships   65
Week 6 Boundaries in Romantic Relationships   79
Week 7 Dealing With Anger and Disappointment   93
Week 8 Dealing With Your Unleashed Emotions   105
Week 9 Effective Ways to Communicate Your Boundaries   114
Week 10 Seven Golden Rules to Better Self-Care   126

Conclusion   *140*
References   *144*

INTRODUCTION

It was nearly midnight and Sandy was still crunching numbers. She could hardly keep her eyes open, but there was no time to sleep. Sandy agreed to take on the responsibility of the budget for the charity she is volunteering at and can't let them down. How did she even end up getting involved in the charity, she asks herself. Then she remembers that she was only planning to go there once when her friend, Peter, asked her to come with him to see what it was all about. Strangely, Peter never returned. In fact, she wonders how he is doing because she hasn't heard from him in months, and yet, here she is taking care of the budget for a charity organization that she doesn't really care for—if she is honest with herself—simply because she continues to say yes to everyone.

As the illuminated numbers on her clock jump to a new day, she realizes that she needs to get up in about four hours, and she hasn't even touched her bed yet. When her friend, Dyna, asked her for help with setting up the venue before their company's annual general meeting, Sandy knew it was going to be a tight fit timewise to get to the city in time that early in the morning, but she didn't know how to say no. Now, she doesn't have a choice. She has made certain commitments, and she needs to stick to them. She just doesn't have any idea how she is going to get through her day. She is so tired and the window of possibility to get any sleep is narrowing at a rapid pace.

It is during the darkest hours of the night that Sandy hits rock bottom. Her physical exhaustion is pressing on her emotional and mental state, and she feels tears well up inside. If only she can say no, but it is so hard. Sandy realizes that everyone will always run to her for help and support, and for the longest time that made her feel wanted, but now she has come to realize that they only ask her because they know her answer is never no. If only she can say no, but how will she ever do that, especially now that everyone already knows she always agrees?

Can you identify with Sandy? How much of your precious time do you spend doing things you don't really care for, and far less benefit from simply because you failed to identify the need for boundaries in your life? The lack of boundaries doesn't only present itself as a problem in time management but also in relationships, may that be romantic, with friends, or family. How many wonderful occasions or opportunities have you missed out on, or said no to by default as you've already agreed to someone or something else?

Every time you say yes, to something or someone, you are saying no to someone or something else, and that is what Sarri Gilman warns us about in the next chapter. The things you say yes and no to are what shape your life, determine the state of your relationships, future, and the level of success and contentment you'll enjoy in life.

In Sandy's case, having set some boundaries would've kept her protected from burnout. However, as we explore the topic in greater depth throughout the book, you'll notice that there are many more areas in life where having boundaries can benefit you. Yes, by following the practical steps set out in a weekly work schedule, you'll become a master in setting and protecting your boundaries. These are not boundaries to block people out of your life, but rather structures to protect what is important to you.

By setting and maintaining boundaries, you can better manage your time to free up some space in your hectic schedule. This is time you can use to gain a greater sense of your identity and to focus on supporting your holistic well-being. The time during which you can build your self-esteem and define and work towards the future you like.

It was later that day that it all changed for Sandy when she finally realized she can't put off making changes to her life any longer. She was stuck on the freeway on her way home after another long and desperately exhausting day committed to taking care of all the responsibilities others tasked her with. She fell asleep behind the steering wheel of her car. Fortunately for Sandy, she only hit the car ahead of her and nobody sustained any serious injuries, but the incident was surely a wake-up call in her life.

Do you need a wake-up call too before you jump to action and bring the change you need? Do you have to wait for something to give, to break, or to happen first? You know your life lacks boundaries, right? You know what you need to do, so what are you waiting for?

Just like many others before you, you too can enjoy the benefits of taking the necessary steps to define the necessary boundaries, establish them in your life, and maintain them to enjoy lasting results.

In this book, I am sharing simple but effective steps to help you along this journey toward freedom and empowerment to enjoy greater confidence and satisfaction in your life. Over the next 10 weeks, you'll learn all you need to know about boundaries. This book provides you with plenty of practical examples to apply to your life and questions to direct you to identify the critical areas in your life, and what steps you need to take right away.

The only question you need to ask yourself now is, "What am I still waiting for?"

Ready to jump in and change your life? Let's go!

WEEK 1:

WHAT ARE BOUNDARIES?

Your story is being shaped by what you are saying yes to and what you are saying no to. —Sarri Gilman

Jenna's frown on her forehead grows deeper and deeper. Regardless of how she tries to shuffle her to-do list, it simply doesn't seem to come together in a workable order. Just one look at the cobweb of black ink in Jenna's journal is a clear statement that she has completely overloaded herself with responsibilities. First, she tried to rearrange her plans for the week by drawing arrows to indicate new time slots for everything on her to-do list before switching to scratching things out and writing them in new spots.

Her weekly schedule is filled with meetings with two new clients—she needs the business, so these two are the only two appointments she doesn't try to rearrange. Then there is her presentation that needs to be done for one of her oldest clients—he is just so loyal, she can't let him down. The school asked her to take charge of the arrangement of the spring dance—she can't say no to that. I mean, what kind of mother refuses to help at her kids' school, right?

The book club ladies are meeting this week at her home, so she needs to clean up a bit and prepare snacks for the ladies. The last time it was at Sylvia's house and all the ladies gossiped about her dirty bathroom and that the snacks were on the skimpy side—she'll die if she hears them say anything like that when she is the hostess. Then there are more meetings, more reports, more proposals, more school responsibilities, and social responsibilities, and then her phone brings her back to reality.

"Charles! Oh, my word! I forgot Honey, I am on my way." She apologizes to her husband as she completely forgot that she had to pick him up from the airport, and then the two will be heading out to see a house they want to buy.

- Does this resemble your life in any way?

- Do you feel swamped by responsibilities?

- Do you have too much on your plate?

- And is it the case that your journal is burdened with activities, responsibilities, and meetings quite simply because you don't say no to anything?

If it is the case, your life is in desperate need to set some boundaries in place.

BOUNDARIES DEFINED

Understanding the term *boundaries* as a physical barrier between two nations, provinces, or states, even between your yard and the neighbors is quite straightforward. But what do boundaries mean when we refer to setting boundaries in your personal life, relationships, work, with your parents, partner, or even kids?

Essentially, the term boundaries doesn't imply anything much different in these scenarios or bonds than when we refer to the barrier setting two nations apart. Boundaries refer to a mental limit between yourself and any other person to clearly indicate where your interest ends and that of the other person starts. It depends on knowing what belongs to you and what does not.

In this context, *belonging* refers to what is yours. So, it will refer to your property, personal space, responsibilities, rights, freedom, responsibilities, and choices, naming only a few factors that are influenced by boundaries. Boundaries are essential to sustain a balanced life and healthy relationships.

BOUNDARIES ARE NOT...

As important as it is to know what boundaries are, is to know what they're not. The term is often misunderstood, and it can even be a concept that leaves some people feeling a bit insecure. This insecurity is mainly the result of misunderstanding the meaning of boundaries. Thus, before we go any further, I want to make it clear that the following are not healthy boundaries.

THEY ARE NOT RULES SET IN STONE

I believe that we all do the best we can with the knowledge we have and as we gain more knowledge and know better, we do better. Coupled with the fact that—ideally—we are continuously growing and evolving, meaning our perspectives, dreams, and wishes change, and so should our boundaries.

Thus, it is highly likely that you establish and communicate boundaries that are relevant to your life today and the knowledge you have in a certain regard. But then once your life evolves and your situation changes, you would want the freedom to change your boundaries as well to keep up with the progress you are making. It is why you need to ensure that your boundaries are flexible, and you can adjust them when necessary.

BOUNDARIES AREN'T LIMITATIONS

There are two perspectives on boundaries or barriers, and it depends entirely on which side of the boundary you are standing on; just consider the fence around your home. For intruders, this fence is an obstruction, keeping them off your property. Hence, they aren't in favor of the structure.

However, you are on the inside of the fence and feel safe once you are behind it. You are content with the fact that the fence keeps intruders out and protects what you value, which can be your loved ones or your property. Thus, you are in favor of having a fence.

When you set boundaries in your life, it is not to keep yourself trapped in a certain zone. No, it is not about limiting your possibilities, but all about protecting what you value in life.

BOUNDARIES AREN'T A WAY TO MANIPULATE OTHERS

I am saying this again: boundaries are tools you should use to protect yourself and what is valuable to you. By no means should you use boundaries to ensure you always get what you want. It should never serve as a tool for manipulation. Boundaries should be reasonable at all times and result in a win-win situation from which everyone benefits.

THERE ARE NO RIGHT OR WRONG BOUNDARIES

Yes, for sure some guidelines will help you to set effective boundaries that are good as they improve your relationships and bonds. But there is no right or wrong when it comes to boundaries. Everyone has unique circumstances, and you need to do what is best and right for you. As long as a boundary protects what is valuable to you, and it is to the benefit of the other party too, then it is the best boundary for you.

UNHEALTHY BOUNDARIES

While there are no wrong boundaries, you do get unhealthy boundaries. An unhealthy boundary reflects a disregard for your or your values, beliefs, goals, dreams, needs, and wants or for that of another person.

The following are all examples of unhealthy boundaries:

- Disregarding someone's physical boundary by touching them inappropriately.
- Keeping yourself responsible for how other people see things or feel over matters.
- Behaving disrespectfully towards others' opinions, values, or beliefs.
- When you, like Jenna, struggle to say no and take on far more than what you are capable of, or when you refuse to accept it when someone else says no.
- Burdening yourself with fixing everything for everyone in your attempts to keep all happy around you.
- Engaging in non-consensual sexual activities.

While these are only a few examples of unhealthy boundaries, it is already pretty evident from this that unhealthy boundaries can be risky, hurtful towards others, and keep you from experiencing joy and satisfaction in your life.

SETTING BOUNDARIES—A CHALLENGING TASK

Setting boundaries in your life—especially in relationships or areas where there were no boundaries before—is often met with resistance. This may leave you feeling uncomfortable, or as if you are the reason for friction in your relationships. For example, let's say you've always been available to answer your family's every need but once you set boundaries, you may be less prone to helping them to do things so they can take care of themselves. This may result in them slightly resenting you to get you to do things for them again.

Yet, the anticipation of friction isn't the only reason why setting boundaries can be hard.

YOU ARE DRIVEN BY THE DESIRE FOR PERFECTIONISM

Let's say you set very high standards for yourself and are always striving for perfection in all you do as well as in your relationships. In your mind, it may be the case that you consider doing everything for everyone else and being available to all whenever they need you as part of the perfect image you are striving to maintain. Yet, this desire to establish perfectionism in your life can lead to burnout, causing you the likelihood of making mistakes, like Jenna did: forgetting about her husband at the airport.

- Are you driven by perfectionism?

- What has this cost you up to this point in life in the form of stress, anxiety, or even costly mistakes you might have made?

FEAR OF MISSING OUT

The fear of missing out, or as it is widely known, FOMO, can make it harder for you to set boundaries in your life. FOMO is directly linked to the desire to be part of the excitement and adventure, and to remain connected. Boundaries may feel like obstructions between yourself and the things you want to remain connected to. It is why FOMO can be an obstacle when you want to set boundaries in your life.

- Does FOMO keep you from making healthy choices for your life and your future?

- How will FOMO negatively impact your future if you fail to take control of it?

- How has FOMO impacted your life in the past?

SOCIAL CONDITIONING

I am referring here largely to your upbringing and the values that were installed in you. Were you raised to always be available for others? For the longest time, women were raised to believe that they have to set their ideals and dreams on the back burner to support their spouses to achieve their dreams, or to look after their families. If certain beliefs are ingrained into your being, it may be very hard to contradict these beliefs through the choices you are making, like setting boundaries in place.

- What are the social norms you were exposed to during your formative years?

- How did these norms impact your life?

- If it wasn't for these influences, what choices would you've made differently?

- How would these choices have impacted your life?

JENNA'S STORY CONTINUED

Are you ready to check in on Jenna again? When we met Jenna, she was overwhelmed and under severe stress. Yet, she still failed to see that she was in desperate need to make some changes to her life. After forgetting her husband at the airport that day, she still continued in her usual manner. Yes, it was only once she forgot to pick her kids up from school a few weeks later that she realized that she can't continue the way she used to.

Sure, she felt bad about forgetting her children and leaving them stranded in front of the school until long after all the other kids left already, but what made it worse was that they were angry at her and so was her husband. Then, she also got called in by the school principal who posed several uncomfortable questions related to her parenting style.

This was more than enough to push Jenna to change her approach to life, and she ended up in my office. We worked on identifying her values and beliefs, and we identified the people and things she valued and wanted to protect at all costs. It is how we could determine a foundation to work from, deciding what are the matters of little to no interest which she wouldn't attend to anymore.

We also worked on finding the correct phrasing to help her to say no without feeling bad. Yes, sure, this was a long journey for Jenna that stretched over several months, but during her latest visit to my office, it was an entirely different person sitting in front of me.

Jenna testified how she now finds her joy and contentment in being all she could be as a spouse, mother, and entrepreneur. She no longer agreed to events or to take care of arrangements of matters just because she felt she had to. No, now Jenna's life is much less burdened with the unnecessary, and she is comfortable passing on control of certain parts of her business to her staff.

This gives her the freedom to be fully attentive when she is spending time with her loved ones, and she can enjoy being part of a family and a business owner in an entirely new and different way.

QUICK RECAP

- Boundaries may initially appear to be restrictive barriers you set up around yourself. However, their true purpose is to protect the people and things you treasure.

- Boundaries should be mutually beneficial, reasonable, and flexible.

- There are many reasons why you may find it hard to set boundaries for the first time. These reasons are mostly rooted in the social exposure you had especially during your childhood years. But they can also be due to your desire to achieve perfectionism or your fear of missing out on something exciting.

- Nonetheless, once you've identified your values and beliefs, the people, places, and things you want to protect, setting up healthy and effective barriers can contribute to your quality of life in several surprising ways.

24

WEEK 2

WHAT REALLY HAPPENS WHEN OUR BOUNDARIES ARE VIOLATED?

A lack of boundaries invites a lack of respect. —Unknown

Do you have boundaries in place already? If so, is maintaining them a constant task you've given up on and now you allow them to be violated by others? Maintaining boundaries is no easy task, especially if they are experiencing constant resistance from those who simply don't respect your wishes. However, regardless of how hard it is to keep your boundaries intact, the price of having your boundaries violated is far more costly as it diminishes your happiness.

IDENTIFYING BOUNDARY VIOLATIONS

Do you find yourself at times in doubt about whether your boundaries were actually violated or whether thinking so is merely your perception? If this is the case, then you are no stranger to knowing how hard it can be to stand firmly in your convictions while your mind is playing games.

Have you ever felt like someone is disregarding your boundaries, but before you become defensive you get distracted by questions like, "Maybe I am just too sensitive?" During these moments you may even try to convince yourself that no action is necessary as "It is okay. I don't want to cause any bad vibes."

Failure to protect your boundaries may bring about certain short-term benefits, but the long-term consequences can severely impact your emotional, physical, and mental health.

The following questions will help you determine whether you are a victim of boundary violations. Your answers should provide you with the necessary certainty to step up and protect what you treasure.

- Do you feel that others tend to take advantage of you?

- Are your emotions used against you for the gain of others?

- Are you constantly finding yourself in the middle of pointless arguments?

- Are you spending a lot of time "saving" those near you, or resolving problems they could've handled themselves?

- Are you constantly defending yourself, your thoughts, ideas, or actions?

- Do your relationships levitate between amazing and terrible while there is no middle ground in between?

- Are you more invested in people and relationships than they are invested in you?

How many of these questions did you answer yes to? Even if it was only a few of these questions you had to agree to, it is still an indication that you are struggling with boundary violations and need to act quickly to get this protective barrier in place to serve you effectively.

SIGNS INDICATING YOUR BOUNDARIES ARE CROSSED

Boundary violations are mostly accompanied by several signs either before they present themselves or while they are taking place.

SIGN #1: YOU NEED TO REPEATEDLY SET THE SAME BOUNDARIES

Are you finding yourself in a cycle of clearly communicating your boundaries to those around you, finding them violated, setting them again, communicating them again, and so the cycle continues? The need to constantly state, defend, adjust, and reaffirm your boundaries is linked to boundary violations. If this is the position you find yourself in, you can be sure that your suspicions are true.

SIGN #2: YOU ARE EXPOSED TO CODEPENDENT BEHAVIOR

What does codependency mean? In simple terms, it means that one person in the relationship—a friendship, romantic relationship, or even a child-parent bond—is placing their wants, needs, and desires on the back burner to attend to the needs of the other. While it is quite common for partners to pause on their dreams and goals to assist the other, it should never be just the same partner whose plans are halted. In a healthy relationship, both partners will at times be advantaged and, at other times, take a step back to make room for their loved one's ideals to enjoy preference.

SIGN #3: SOMETHING FEELS OFF

You can't put your finger on exactly what you are feeling, but you know for sure that something just doesn't feel right. It can be that your relationship is making you feel trapped, unsafe, or even nervous.

SIGN #4: YOUR REQUESTS ARE MOCKED OR DISMISSED

You are attending to all the needs of the other person in this relationship to the best of your capabilities, but when you request something, your requests aren't heard, quickly forgotten, dismissed, or, even worse, laughed at.

SIGN #5: YOUR EXISTENCE IS HARDLY ACKNOWLEDGED

When you express your feelings, it isn't acknowledged by the other person, and it is almost as if they don't hear you at all. It is one thing to have your requests dismissed, but not having your feelings heard is an entirely different hurtful matter.

While there are many more indications that your boundaries are under constant threat, these five signs are quite common and surely serve as an indication of the existing disregard for your boundaries.

THE IMPACT OF BOUNDARY VIOLATIONS

The damaging effect of boundary violations affects your mental, emotional, and physical wellness.

Your brain is first in the firing line when it comes to such violations. Initially, the violation will be recognized by your *amygdala*. This is a small part of the brain, shaped like two almonds, which is responsible for your most basic survival. However, the limbic system also has a role to play. The latter is in charge of emotional management, and it also controls the fear response which is mainly activated by the amygdala.

The initial reaction when your mind realizes that your boundaries have been crossed is to go into the fight, flight, or freeze response. While this is a rather dramatic response impacting you mentally, emotionally, and physically, you may not notice it straight away. Yes, many people go into this state without even realizing the state of despair their minds and bodies are in, and it is only later on that they start to suffer serious health concerns.

Nonetheless, once the brain responds in a specific manner, the body will show signs of distress too.

On a physical level, you can expect to observe the following changes in your health:

- Your body physically prepares itself to fight, and your heart rate will speed up.

- Simultaneously, your blood pressure increases and your breathing becomes more rapid and shallow.

- Muscles tend to tense up to improve your performance in any physical fights.

These are all common symptoms of your body preparing yourself to perform well in the face of any threat you are exposed to. And similar to being in a high-stress environment for extended periods, being in a state of stress for long periods has a detrimental impact on your overall health and wellness.

Yes, having your boundaries violated places you in the same stressful situation caused by any other high-stress scenario and can lead to chronic high blood pressure, poor heart health, diabetes, insomnia, and a weaker immune system.

- Are you currently experiencing elevated stress levels?
- Have you noticed changes in your overall wellness that may be indicative of the presence of such high prevailing stress levels?

CONSEQUENCES OF LIFE WITHOUT BOUNDARIES

Having your boundaries violated is stressful and has a detrimental impact on your overall well-being, but what is even worse is a life without having any boundaries in place.

Living life this way is mostly synonymous with experiencing constant high levels of stress and anxiety as you are always concerned that you'll be letting someone down along the way.

DRAMATIC RELATIONSHIPS

Do you find that your relationships are often difficult to endure and the mere drama associated with them is draining you? This is most likely due to your lack of boundaries. Remember that people will always treat you the way you show them is acceptable to treat you. If you are going to attach little to no value to your goals and dreams, they will too.

In the same manner, if you are going to teach others that you are always available to tend to their every need and are open to being taken advantage of, they most likely will. If this is the case in your life, it surely is time to consider getting at least some boundaries in place.

YOUR MIND IS BURIED IN A CLOUD OF ANNOYANCE

Do you find yourself being annoyed most of the time and at times you'll even act out but you do so with passive aggression? Feeling this way is normal as you are overwhelmed by the problems and needs of others that they expect you to attend to or resolve on their behalf. As you still fail to set any boundaries and continue to allow the manipulation to take place, you start to reflect the negative energy you are exposed to back to others.

Yet, you don't do this by stating clearly that you are no longer willing to continue this way. You rather opt for a passive-aggressive approach to shed some of your frustration with your situation. As you are still not doing anything to improve the state you are in, this approach is not going to bring about any improvement in your life.

YOUR HIDDEN FEAR IS THAT YOU'LL BE REJECTED

The need to belong is part of human nature. We are born with the desire to be part of something larger than ourselves.

Therefore, the fear of rejection can be debilitating. As you are convinced that once you set boundaries in place, others will reject you when you do, you continue to disregard your own value, just to keep others happy and not reject you.

Sure, if you've surrounded yourself with people who are only out there to use you and to see what you can do for them, they'll surely reject you when you set boundaries in place. But these were not people who ever truly cared about you, and you are better off without them. The ones who do truly care about you will understand your need to protect what is precious to you. In this manner, setting boundaries will help you to clear your life from those who are only there for the free ride they get simply by knowing you.

YOU ARE GUILTY OF OVERSHARING

In modern terms, we refer to oversharing as *TMI* or *too much information.* It boils down to your inability to distinguish what information is necessary and good to share, and which details about your life should rather be kept to yourself. People who lack boundaries in their lives don't have any guidelines regarding what information is best kept private.

YOU'VE LOST YOUR IDENTITY

When you are so immersed in helping others to realize their dreams and goals, and you are constantly placing your needs and desires on the back burner, it is only normal that at some point you may no longer know exactly who you are, or what you want to achieve in life. Remember that for as long as you are attending to the needs of everyone else and working towards making their dreams come true, nobody is attending to your needs, and, at some point, you are bound to feel that you have lost track of your identity.

- Which of the above signs are present in your life?

- Except for these signs, can you observe any other indications in your life that you are too involved in the lives of others and too little present working on your goals and dreams?

- What will your future look like if you still don't put any boundaries in place?

SALLY'S STORY

Suddenly Sally has the urge to pull over her truck on the highway. As the vehicle comes to an abrupt stop next to the road, Sally slams the steering wheel a couple of times, screams out loud, and falls back in her seat, just breathing deeply for a bit.

While she appears to be completely calm on the outside now, her mind is racing. She always feels this way after she visits her mom, but lately, it is only getting worse. Sally lives about an hour's drive away from her mom. She is the elderly lady's only child and the only living relative she has left. Therefore, Sally has always been very committed to meeting her mom's every need.

However, Sally's mom is using Sally's commitment to her well-being against her daughter and in favor of herself. As Sally is very busy building her business while being a mom of three toddlers, she has had little time to attend to her mother's needs lately.

The older woman doesn't like this at all. When she feels that Sally is neglecting her, she would always revert to late-night phone calls, causing nothing but distress for Sally. Last night, Sally got a call around 11 pm. This call kept her from sleeping and urged her to get into her truck before the crack of dawn to attend to Mom's needs. When Sally arrived at her mother's home, none of the things she complained about the previous night were present. She merely played on her daughter's emotions for attention.

When Sally confronted her mom about her lies, her mother refused to say any of the things that Sally accuses her of and insisted that her daughter is lying to be mean to her old mother. Sally has no defense when she is accused of lying or even imagining things. What Sally experiences is the effect of having a gaslighter in her life, but Sally hasn't realized yet that her mom has been guilty of it for her entire life.

WHY OTHERS CROSS YOUR BOUNDARIES

Gaslighting is one way for others to overstep your boundaries. Other ways are lying, nagging, or harassing. It also happens when people take advantage of you based on the power they have, their age, gender, or financial status.

These are all awful ways to treat someone you pretend to love, but why do people do it?

LACK OF CLEAR BOUNDARIES

It can be that you haven't stated your boundaries clearly enough. When you fail to express exactly what your boundary entails, it may be murky to some, and they'll cross it at times by accident.

YOU DIDN'T STATE THE CONSEQUENCES

You may also not have made it clear that there will be consequences when others overstep your boundaries, or if there are consequences, you are likely not enforcing them when necessary. By neglecting to see it through if your boundaries were crossed, you are passively telling others that these consequences are merely empty threats and contain no meaning. It comes across that you aren't serious about your boundaries or the implications if others don't respect them.

LACK OF CONSISTENCY

Your boundaries may not be consistent enough. If you are constantly changing your boundaries, or show that you are lenient when it comes to setting these limits around your life, others will consider your boundaries merely as a suggestion and not as something they should respect.

BOUNDARIES ARE UNFAIR OR UNREASONABLE

Your boundaries may also be unfair or unreasonable. Remember that boundaries are never to be used to manipulate others and should always lead to mutual benefit.

YOU ARE DEALING WITH A NARCISSIST, GASLIGHTER, OR MANIPULATOR

Then, in the most extreme cases, people will also disrespect your boundaries because they are narcissists, gaslighters, and manipulators. These are the people who are only in your life because they can benefit from having you around. Even though you may be convinced that you are in a mutually caring relationship, this is not the case. What makes this even worse is sometimes these relationships can be romantic relationships with a partner you truly care about, or even with a parent, like Sally's mom.

QUICK RECAP

- Do you suspect that your boundaries are being violated? Familiarize yourself with the signs indicating others are crossing your boundaries to know this for sure.

- The impact of having your boundaries crossed isn't merely restricted to your mental health but also impacts your physical wellness in the same manner as exposure to high-stress situations does.

- While the symptoms of having your boundaries crossed are quite severe, the impact of having no boundaries set is even worse. The lack of boundaries will affect every aspect of your life, from your relationships to your overall sense of joy and satisfaction in life.

- There are many ways in which others will cross your boundaries, and there are as many reasons why they do.

- These reasons vary from you not expressing your boundaries with clarity and conviction to them being narcissists with no inherent respect for the boundaries of others.

WEEK 3

WHAT REALLY HAPPENS IF YOU ALLOW YOUR BOUNDARIES TO TAKE CARE OF YOU

Boundaries are basically about providing structure, and structure is essential in building anything that thrives. — Henry Cloud

Does the idea of having access to a powerful tool that will help you flourish in life excite you? Are you keen to learn all about the steps you need to take to access the life you've been dreaming about? One of the stranger aspects of human nature is that we tend to believe that the more complex a solution is, the more effective it would be.

If this is a statement you can identify with, I might disappoint you now. There is truly nothing complex about setting boundaries in place to protect what you value. Later on, we'll discuss the process in much greater detail, but, for now, I want to expand on how these boundaries can improve your quality of life.

Setting boundaries in life can transform your life in the present and future. Yet, the idea is often met with a strong sense of reluctance and disbelief as it is such a simplistic quest.

BETTER BOUNDARIES MEANS A BETTER YOU

Regardless of how hard you try, you can't be the *be-all* and *do-all* for everyone in your life. Sure, there might be the expectation that you are, but by setting up the necessary boundaries to protect your limited resources—like your time—you'll put an end to these expectations and make your life way easier and more enjoyable.

GROWTH IN SELF-AWARENESS

Before you can set any boundaries, you need to invest time in yourself to determine what your goals and dreams are. What are your values and beliefs? Many people simply go through life without ever pondering these matters. They are so busy maintaining their lives that they never have time to live or even plan their futures. However, once you set boundaries, you have to become more self-aware as you need to identify first what exactly is important enough to you to want to protect it.

HEALTHIER RELATIONSHIPS

One of the common symptoms of a lack of boundaries is that too often you find yourself tied down by the many things you've agreed to do. While doing these things doesn't contribute to your life in any manner, it does tap all your energy resources, leaving you depleted with nothing to contribute to your relationships. Thus, once you start to protect your time and energy by setting up boundaries, you have time to recharge and can contribute more to the important relationships you have, helping these bonds to grow even stronger.

REDUCE YOUR STRESS

Does the idea of not helping someone leave you feeling stressed and anxious? Perhaps it is the fact that you don't know when you are going to fit all you need to take care of into your schedule that is causing your stress levels to remain unhealthily high. Regardless of what causes you to experience this, having proper strong boundaries in place reduces the risk of over-extending yourself as well as the pressure others place on you.

GREATER COMPASSION

The more you start to care for yourself and have compassion for your needs and feelings, the more your awareness of the needs and feelings of others starts to grow, enabling you to show more compassion to those around you.

FIVE AMAZING BENEFITS OF HEALTHY BOUNDARIES

It is not only your overall wellness that improves when you have healthy boundaries in place, but also your relationships, approach to life, your obstacles, and your perspective on the future.

LESS CONFLICT TO DEAL WITH

Conflict is mostly an energy-sapping waste of time. How often are the arguments you are involved in caused by poor communication skills and misunderstandings? Under such circumstances, arguments can occur over the most insignificant matters.

When you have clear boundaries in place, and you inform others about these boundaries while also maintaining them when they are challenged, you make your viewpoints very clear. It is how you make it easy for others to know where they stand with you and what you are willing to do to benefit your relationship. Boundaries create the perfect foundation to have clear communication that reduces the possibility of conflict.

BOUNDARIES MAKE SAYING NO MUCH EASIER

It can be so hard for some to simply say *no*. We've already touched on that in chapter one with Jenna's story and the challenges she was facing due to her inability to say no. You may feel that you are going to be disliked or rejected if you do.

Sometimes it can even happen that you have decided that you won't agree to do certain things again, but once you least expect it to happen, you are asked and are caught off guard. As you lack a plan on how to respond in these instances, you simply say yes as that is the familiar course of action. When you have boundaries in place, you have prepared a blueprint of how you will respond in the future and this gives you guidance on how to say no without feeling guilty.

YOU HAVE TIME TO DO WHAT YOU LIKE

When last did you have time to attend to your hobbies? Do you even have a hobby or have you been busy for so long that you've never even thought about getting a hobby, or even worse, had time to think about what you would like to take up as a hobby? Is this lack of time you have due to the many responsibilities you've taken on in your quest to be there for everyone? Boundaries will guide those who are perfectly capable of taking care of some of their own responsibilities themselves away from your limited time resources, freeing up space in your schedule to do what you like.

BOUNDARIES PUT YOU IN THE DRIVING SEAT OF YOUR LIFE

Do you feel like a juggler keeping so many balls in the air there is no time to take one step forward? Yes, taking even the smallest step in a certain direction can be enough of a distraction to cause you to drop everything on the floor. Just imagine the sheer humiliation of going through something like that.

Once you've established what you want to safeguard with your boundaries, set them up, and communicate them clearly to all relevant parties, the number of balls you need to juggle is surely going to become fewer. This means that you can progress in life, determine what direction you want to go, and take one step at a time to where you want to be.

IMPROVES YOUR HOLISTIC WELLNESS

From the benefits that we've discussed so far, it is clear having boundaries in place will always have a holistic positive impact on your life. These benefits may originally occur in a certain chosen area, but soon you'll see they ripple out and improve vastly more of your life than what you've envisioned.

For example, let's say you want to protect your time with your boundaries as you feel everyone at the office is just popping into your office whenever they are facing the most insignificant challenge, and they expect you to take care of it on their behalf even though they are perfectly capable of taking care of it themselves.

You clearly communicate that you'll only be available at certain times and if they want to see you, they need to make an appointment. Suddenly, it isn't so easy to just pop in and waste your time, so this happens less often. You get to have more time to focus on what you need to do.

Now, your work is done by the end of the day, and you don't have to work late anymore. As you are home earlier, you have time to attend the art classes around the corner. You are feeling more relaxed, and have time to think about your life and where your future is heading. Your health improves and so do your mental and emotional state as your life is now far more balanced.

- Does this sound like the kind of improvement you want or need to see in your life?

- Which of these mentioned benefits sound the most alluring to you right now?

- Why is that the case? What do you need to do right now to improve your situation?

BOUNDARIES EQUAL BETTER COMMUNICATION

It is important that you clearly communicate your boundaries to others, but the relationship between boundaries and communication is far more complex than that. Boundaries also have an impact on the way you communicate.

It is vital to adjust your communication style to express your boundaries with clarity and as you have to adopt a more effective way of communicating, your overall style of communication improves.

When you state your boundaries, there are several key elements you need to include in your communication.

- You need to clearly explain what the boundary entails. This is normally something along the lines of setting a condition and then a response. Examples would be:
    - ☐ Only if you have tried to do this several times and are still struggling, you are allowed to ask me for help.
    - ☐ You can always rely on me, but you'll have to wait until I can fit you in.
    - ☐ During weekends, spending time with my family is my priority, so please don't contact me with work-related inquiries during this time.
- Next, you need to make it clear that there will be consequences if these boundaries aren't respected.
    - ☐ If I am being contacted over the weekend regarding a work-related matter, I will still only respond on Mondays.
- Use "I" statements to make it clear that you've made the decision and that you'll take the necessary action. This way of speaking is evident in the above example.
- Lastly, keep in mind that your boundaries may still be tested and when it happens you need to stick to your

decisions. Even if you see that there are work-related emails in your inbox, don't open them until Monday, and only take care of these matters as per your stipulations. Remember that if you aren't going to stick to what you've stipulated as the consequences of violations of your boundaries, nobody will.

Once you're in the habit of communicating clearly in this regard, you'll find that it is much easier to express yourself with clarity in many other scenarios.

- How would you describe your current ability to communicate effectively?

- Which improvements would you like to see in this regard?

BOUNDARIES REFLECTING LOVE AND RESPECT FOR OURSELVES

One of life's harder lessons is that people treat us the way we allow them to treat us. I guess we can also say people treat us the way we show them they can treat us.

If your actions and ways of speaking are reflecting a lack of self-respect, then others won't treat you with respect either. But if you use your boundaries to indicate what you are willing to do and what not, and that you attach value to your ideas, opinions, and goals, others will gradually begin to treat you similarly.

And if they don't? Then your boundaries will simply keep them at a distance, and they'll never be allowed near you. It is how you can make more room for those who genuinely care about your well-being and success in your life.

Setting boundaries is a way to show respect to yourself and to show others how you want them to respect you as a person too. Even more importantly though is that boundaries can also serve as an effective way to determine who are the people you want to have in your life, and who are merely tagging along as you offer them a free ride.

- When was the last time you felt that someone wasn't treating you with the respect you deserve? Describe the situation.

- Which image did the way you treated yourself reflect to that person?

- Is it possible that the way you treated yourself guided that person to treat you a certain way?

- What can you do better next time?

DAPHNE'S STORY

Daphne is one of the three-floor managers her company employs to ensure customer care is simply outstanding in the cosmetics department. The other two ladies are quite close friends with each other but also with the store manager who appointed them to these positions.

Company policy states that the three ladies need to take turns on who is going to take leave during the holidays. While the other two ladies have families at home, Daphne is single and has no kids at all. Her parents also passed away several years ago, so she doesn't have family gatherings to attend during the festive season. It means that every year, the other two ladies request leave for this time already early on, and as they are friends with the store manager, they get it, even if it was Daphne's time to be off during this time.

For seven years, Daphne has worked every Thanksgiving, Christmas, and Easter. This year, she wants to travel to New York to experience Christmas in the city. She applied for leave already early on and, legally, her manager was bound to approve it. Then, as per usual, the two ladies started to approach Daphne, nudging her to see if she'll change her plans.

While Daphne would usually give in to their requests as she was concerned that they won't like her if she doesn't, this year is different. This year Daphne has set boundaries, and she is communicating them clearly the moment she sees her two coworkers heading her way with their mission to get the relief they are so used to every year.

She tells them that her tickets and accommodation are already booked and that it is time for her to take care of her own needs. Yes, she understands that they have families, and she doesn't, but that she still has a life and dreams for this time of year, and this time around, she is giving her needs and desires preference. While she is willing to help them out in the future when it is suitable for her, this won't be the case this time around. She also expressed her intention to take off over the holidays in the future as per her contract stipulations.

However, this wasn't the last time that her boundaries in this regard were tested. No, even her store manager asked her if she would reconsider. Fortunately, Daphne has studied her agreement and determined that if she doesn't take off, as per company policy, the store can get into trouble with the group of companies.

For the first time in years, Daphne was showing others the level of respect she wants to be treated with. She showed even her superior that she is entitled to take time off during this time of the year and that she is willing to stand up for this right.

Once Daphne started showing others that she deserves to be respected, everyone started to treat her like someone they value. It wasn't long after the season was over that the company's regional manager paid them a visit, and not only was the store manager transferred to another store, but Daphne was also promoted to be the new store manager.

QUICK RECAP

- Having healthy boundaries in place improves your life in every single area. You'll enjoy greater self-awareness, more confidence, more free time, less stress, and enjoy better health.

- There is a complex relationship between communication and boundaries. You need to communicate your boundaries clearly and effectively, but as you learn how to do that, you also become better skilled in communicating clearly for every aspect of your life. Better communication results in fewer misunderstandings, friction, and confrontations.

- Boundaries are a way to show others that you respect yourself and that you expect the same from them. It is a way to show others how you want them to treat you.

WEEK 4

MASTER YOUR PERSONAL BOUNDARY SKILLS

You are not required to set yourself on fire to keep others warm. —Unknown

Do you continue to cut yourself short, shift your goals to the background, and devalue your needs and wants? Were you raised to believe that it is the right thing to do? Are you under the impression that it is the only way to make friends? Do you perhaps fear that if you stop doing it, you will be rejected, despised, or even worse perhaps, gossiped over?

Maybe the description above is quite accurately capturing the person you used to be. But now you are ready to make the transition in your life to prioritize yourself for a change. However, this change demands that you shift some of your established perspectives in life. Only once you've done that can you take the first step to make progress in the right direction.

BOUNDARIES AND SELF-SACRIFICE

One of the most common misunderstandings linked to boundaries is that they are intended to keep others out, or even to keep you locked into a little safe zone. This perception of boundaries is entirely wrong. Grant me a moment to illustrate that this perception of boundaries isn't only wrong, but is also giving it a bad reputation.

Let's compare the boundaries you set in your life to the boundary walls you would use to protect your yard. Before you had this wall up, your yard and home were completely open and exposed. Anyone could enter your property of free will and without restriction. If someone wanted to dump their trash on your lawn, they could. If they saw your magnificent roses, nothing was stopping them from walking up to your rose bushes and just taking what they wanted. Even your property in your home wasn't safe as anyone could walk up to your windows, break in, and take what they wanted.

One day you decide that you've had enough of this, and you decide to build a boundary wall around your yard. This will keep unlawful trespassers and thieves off your property and away from your treasured roses. Sure, building such a structure will surely be a concern for those who just came and went onto your property as they pleased, but for you and your loved ones, this boundary wall is a blessing. You feel safer and secure in your home and you enjoy much greater privacy. You have control over who you let in through your gate and this way, you can better manage what is happening in your yard and your home. Finally, you are the master of the property you've been investing so much in.

Do you feel that your wall is keeping you captured? No, of course not. You simply exist through the gate, right? Similarly, you still have control over who you let through your gates and onto your property. These may still be people who have some of your roses, and you may want to give them some as you are generous by nature, but now you have control over who you allow to share your time and effort.

This is exactly how boundaries in life work, and setting up these boundaries will leave some people upset as they don't have unrestricted access to you anymore. They can't just take and demand whatever they like at the time when they do so. Yet, it doesn't mean that you won't be able to help anyone any longer. No, it just means that you have control over who you help, when you do so, and what you are willing to do.

When you set up boundaries in your life, you can still be very much willing to sacrifice your time, money, effort, talents, attention, or any other skill or possession you are willing to use to help a fellow human being, but you no longer do this at the cost of your dreams, ideals, values, needs, beliefs, or goals.

You can still be there for your loved ones, but you are taking greater care to ensure that you don't get hurt in the process while you ensure that your mental, physical, and emotional well-being is cared for first. This is not a selfish act. If you continue to pour from your cup until you have nothing left to give, you won't be able to make any meaningful contribution to anyone. But if you take care of yourself first, if you recharge and recuperate regularly behind the safety of your boundaries, you are of much more value to those who need you, when they need you the most.

FIRST STEP: CREATE BOUNDARIES

I am going to assume that at this stage you haven't set any boundaries yet and that your life is like a yard without a fence. All you are certain of is that you need some boundaries, but you may still be unsure about what exactly it is you would want to achieve by doing so.

WHAT DO YOU WANT TO KEEP SAFE?

The very first step would be to identify what it is that you would like to protect. Is it your values that you feel are severely challenged by family and friends? Perhaps it is your time that people have no regard for.

- Grab a pen and paper and list the aspects of your life that you need to protect or keep safe.

- Once you have your list together, determine why these things are so important to you that you feel the need to keep them safe with boundaries.

- What are the boundaries you would need to set up to ensure the safety of these things?

- Can you identify circumstances or requests where you have no other choice than saying no?

- Why is it that you feel you have to say no under these circumstances?

- How will these changes impact your relationships?

- What makes these relationships different from others so that you feel they will be more largely impacted?

Now, let's put your suggested boundaries under the microscope.

- Are the boundaries fair?

- Do they ensure a mutually beneficial outcome?

- Are they realistic?

- Do they protect your needs entirely?

- Are you sure that these boundaries are necessary and fair and not set up in a manner to manipulate others?

CALVIN'S STORY

Calvin is an only child and since his dad passed away, his mother drew closer to him to the point where she became extremely needy and wanted his attention all the time. Initially, Calvin felt sorry for his mother, but later on, the amount of time she demanded from him to take care of matters, which she was perfectly fit to do herself, became too much. She would often request him on short notice to come to her aid, and there have been times when he even had to cancel his plans to accommodate her.

She even started nagging him to get rid of his apartment in the city where he and his wife stayed to move in with her. Calvin knew that his mom and wife aren't very fond of each other and that his wife is already getting irritated as he had several times already canceled plans with her too when his mom gave him the impression that she needed him urgently, and once he arrived, nothing serious was wrong.

Calvin realized that he had to set certain boundaries in place. For sure, he loved his mother and wanted to be there for her, but he had to take control over when he would do this, otherwise his entire life would begin to unravel.

He valued the fact that he was a good son to his mother and wanted to be there for her in her time of need. But he also valued the fact that he is a great spouse for his wife, and he wants her to feel that he is prioritizing her and their relationship too.

His solution was to reach out to his mom's neighbor, a lady who was also a widow but somewhat younger than his mom. The lady agreed that if his mother is ever phoning him to complain about a crisis that he needs to sort out immediately, the lady will step in to judge for herself how serious the matter truly is. He also decided that every second weekend, he would pop in at his mom's place on a Saturday morning to see if there is anything she needs. She should use the time in between to gather a list of all the things he had to take care of and send him the list on the day before he would come around so that he could already get things he might need. For example, one tap was dripping, and he could get the necessary parts on his way there to fix the tap.

Once Calvin was sure his boundaries would work effectively, he was ready to move on to the second stage of the process: communicating it clearly to the relevant people.

SECOND STEP: START COMMUNICATING ASSERTIVELY

First, Calvin presented his plans to his wife to be sure that she agrees with him and to get her input as they are a team. She agreed and was grateful for his willingness to address this concern. Next, he had to present his newly established boundaries to his mother and he knew that this would be a greater challenge to get to run smoothly.

Before he sat down with his mom, Calvin considered the following guidelines.

BOUNDARIES SHOULD NEVER HURT ANOTHER

Never use your boundaries to hurt people or to get back to them. Sure, you may feel so frustrated with them as they've placed you in a position where you needed to act, but ultimately you are establishing these boundaries intending to benefit both parties. For Calvin, these boundaries meant that he could still help his mother but not at the cost of his relationship with his wife, or his own dreams, responsibilities, and balanced life.

TAKE OWNERSHIP OF YOUR BOUNDARIES

He knew that he had to choose his words wisely not to offend his mother, and he had to make it clear that it was his idea, not his wife's. Once Calvin and his mother sat down to have a cup of coffee, he complimented her on how well she had managed since his father's passing. He felt that reminding her what she is capable of will remove her learned helplessness she has been portraying for a while.

PICK YOUR TIMING WISELY

She immediately took his bait and this created the perfect setting to tell her that he is claiming his life back, and that while he will always love her and be there for her, but he just can't be there for her any time of the day or night. He reminded her that she raised him well and that he has a life that also demands his attention. Then, he shared his plans and assured her that he will be popping in as promised, and that if she truly needs someone urgently, her neighbor is always willing to assist.

He also stated that expects his mother to respect his wishes and that he is sure that she'll cooperate in this regard. He made it clear that even if she doesn't, he will not come around for no good reason at all. If she's angry at him because of this choice, then it is her problem, not his, to deal with.

PROVIDE REASONS FOR YOUR CHOICE

While Calvin's mom didn't like one bit what her son just told her, he made such a good argument and considered so many factors, that she soon realized that no counter-argument will change his mind.

EXPECT RESISTANCE

Of course, she tried to push back on his boundaries several times afterward, but Calvin just stuck to his arrangements and gradually his mother realized that it wouldn't work. As he wasn't around so much anymore, she began to shift her attention to other things too. She joined a book club in her neighborhood and started to take walks in the park again. Calvin's boundaries protected what he valued, but also helped his mother to realize and reclaim her own power.

Communicating your boundaries for the very first time can be a very sensitive matter, but as long as you put some thought into how you are going to say it, it will come across. Again, always use "I" statements as they tend to sound less like accusations. Clearly state what your expectations are and what the consequences will be if your wishes aren't respected.

THIRD STEP: WHAT ARE THE CONSEQUENCES

For example, instead of saying, "You are always so rude to me when you are angry," say, "I don't appreciate the way you talk to me when you are angry, and if you can't change that, I'll have to walk away from the conversation until you are calmed down."

You don't only have to express the consequences, you need to stick to them too. So, if you stated that you will take certain actions, you need to stick to this when your boundaries are violated.

If you stated that you will walk away when you are spoken to rudely, you need to walk away when it happens. At that moment, you can assert yourself calmly, communicate clearly the consequences, and act them out.

QUICK RECAP

- Setting boundaries doesn't mean that you are blocking people out of your life, but much rather that you'll still be helping them on your terms.

- When you set boundaries, you need to be clear on what you want to protect, why you want to protect it, and how you think would be the best way to provide this protection.

- The second step would be to communicate your boundaries to the relevant people. Do so calmly but assertively.

- Lastly, be prepared to have your boundaries challenged. When this happens, you need to proceed and follow through on the consequences you've stated.

WEEK 5

BOUNDARIES AND FRIENDSHIPS

The only people who get upset when you set boundaries are those who benefit from you having none. —Unknown

What was supposed to be a quick journey from one city to another turned into an excruciatingly exhausting trip as Dennis's flight was delayed several times due to bad weather.

When the plane finally took off, everyone on board was tired and somewhat irritated. There were a couple of times when turbulence was really bad and this only worsened the mood on board. However, this wasn't the most excruciating part of his journey, a journey that should've lasted less than two hours and by now it is almost 18 hours since he left his home to visit his parents for the Thanksgiving weekend. No, his worst nightmare booked her seat right next to him and her name was Deloris.

Deloris is a talker. He fell for her bait when she offered him some of her chocolate. He was hungry and could surely do with the sugar for energy, and he took a block, a deed he regretted multiple times since. His acceptance served as her cue that he is open to listening to her...for the entire trip...as she was talking non-stop.

The much older woman told him how she can't wait to spend time with her boyfriend this weekend. It was only much later on that he realized the boyfriend was about half her age, and she was going for a conjugal visit at the prison in the city. She told him about how her lover was a friend of her son and that the two got arrested together. Deloris also mentioned how her husband didn't like her son hanging out with him, but that he never approved of anyone anyway. She shared how she fell in love with the young man, how he charmed her, seduced her, and then the conversation took an uncomfortable downward spiral as it was evident that not even the tiniest detail was too much for Deloris to share.

At certain points, it felt for Dennis like the only way he is ever going to get out of this nightmarish hell would be if the plane would go down with the turbulence that managed to keep them all in their seats the entire time. Deloris had no filter, no limits to what is acceptable to share with strangers, and what should rather be kept private.

It was also clear that she would do everything for this young man who is ruling her life from prison. It seems that he got her to pay almost all the money she earns as a waitress at the roadhouse over to him so that he can buy what he needs inside prison. She even lent him her car, which he evidently used as a get-away vehicle. Currently, this is still held in the police pound.

Deloris is a woman who should be in her golden years of life, and yet, she has no idea what she wants to do with her remaining years except to make sure her jailed sweetheart stays true to her.

She lost her identity in life and has no sense of self. She is resentful towards her family as her kids—except for the one who does time with her lover—chose their dad's side and don't want to have anything to do with her. Even though *she gave up her entire life to make sure they were doing okay.*

Deloris had no personal boundaries and while she might not have been aware of it, it was pretty clear that everyone around her knew this.

SIGNS SHOWING YOUR LACK OF PERSONAL BOUNDARIES

Some of the most prominent indications that you lack personal boundaries are:

- You cannot make decisions. For some, even the most insignificant choices can be overwhelming, and they struggle to choose between available options.

- You are a people pleaser and will cut yourself short to keep others happy and content.

- Closely linked to the above point is your tendency to use every minute of your time to serve others.

- You will do this to the point where you have no energy left.

- You take such care to answer to the needs of everyone else, that you lose your own identity along the way, and, eventually, you find yourself at a point where you no longer have any sense of self.

- As this investment in the interest and well-being of others isn't repaid, it is not uncommon to end up feeling resentment towards these people.

- Like Deloris, those who lack personal boundaries are known to overshare even the tiniest details of their lives. They have no idea what information is best kept private as it is not intended for the ears of anyone else.

While these might appear to be all rather obvious concerns, it can be easy to go through life without ever realizing that the string of bad luck following you wherever you go is a direct result of your lacking boundaries.

- Do any of these signs hit uncomfortably close to home for you?

- Perhaps you can see some of these symptoms in your life, or maybe you have someone close to you who needs urgent assistance to set up boundaries in their life.

DETERMINING YOUR PERSONAL BOUNDARIES

What do personal boundaries look like, and how do you identify what boundaries you need to put in place in your life?

The challenge with personal boundaries is that you can easily only consider what boundaries you have to limit the actions of others in your life and seldom think about what boundaries you would set for yourself to make your life easier.

When it comes to setting personal boundaries, you first need to identify how far you can push yourself before it starts hurting, or before you start to feel ashamed or guilty over your actions. Even if you find yourself feeling extremely confused and setting boundaries is exceptionally hard for you, there will always be a point where you know that anything that occurs after this point is painful.

For example, you may be fine with telling white lies to save yourself from humiliation, but when it comes to lying straight to someone else's face, the action leaves you feeling guilty or ashamed, and that equates to hurting and definitely indicates where you need to draw the line.

- Identify what the things are that you are still doing that leave you feeling uncomfortable internally.

- Phrase the boundaries that will protect you from doing these things.

- What do you need to do right away to prevent this from happening again?

ANNE'S STORY

Anne has been friends with Beth since first grade. While Anne would drop everything she is busy with when Beth needs her, Beth seldom—if ever—repays this loyalty she has been used to for about two decades. Except for the fact that Anne is available whenever Beth needs her, she would also mostly take a position in the backseat of their friendship.

Beth's break-ups would be dramatic events that, at times, meant that Anne stayed away from her classes and later on took sick days at work to attend to her friend's broken heart. However, when Anne would go through the same heartache, Beth would be off on a weekend away, have pressing deadlines, and it would be impossible for her to spend time with Anne. Then there was that one occasion when she just simply couldn't come because of a Bloomingdale's sale.

When Beth got engaged, Anne was truly happy for her friend and celebrated her happiness with her, but when Anne got engaged, Beth gave her a shallow "Congrats," and then started to compare the size of the diamonds in their rings.

While it can be so easy to point fingers at Beth, calling her a bad friend, it is also important to notice the fact that maybe Anne is failing here too. She is failing herself due to her lack of boundaries to protect herself in this friendship. As much as Beth is taking advantage of Anne whenever she can, Anne has been allowing this to happen, at times even enabling Beth to behave in this manner, and it is time for her to step up to protect herself.

It is time that Anne realizes that every time she chooses Beth and says yes to her needs, she is cutting herself short and saying no to what is important to her. Anne needs to see that for as long as she reserves Beth's position in her life, she is keeping her time occupied with a friendship that doesn't go both ways and by doing so, she is missing out on the opportunity to make new and hopefully more authentic friendships going both ways.

SETTING BOUNDARIES WITHIN FRIENDSHIPS

From the story above, it is evident that Anne needs to put certain boundaries in place when it comes to her friendship with Beth. The need for boundaries is so evident, it almost feels like you want to scream at her, telling her that she deserves better, right? But then again, it is always easier to see where other people go wrong than to realize the mistakes we make ourselves.

The best boundaries to have in friendships will protect and value your personal space and needs without taking anything away from your friend. It is a way to show that you value yourself, that you consider yourself worthy to be treated a certain way, and that you won't tolerate people in your life—much less in friendships—who don't respect you as a person or as a friend. A well-structured boundary will do all of the above without taking anything away from your friend.

HOW TO SET BOUNDARIES IN FRIENDSHIPS

If you are like Anne and are also involved in a one-sided friendship with someone who never appreciates the value you add to the relationship, it may feel like setting boundaries to protect your space and needs would be selfish. It is even possible that the other person would want you to believe that this is the case, and this approach from someone you consider to be a friend will make it even harder to set your boundaries.

- Have you ever thought about what you consider to be okay to happen in your relationships with friends?

- What do you consider as unacceptable in these friendship bonds?

- Have friends ever violated your boundaries?

- If so, why did it happen? Did you set boundaries or merely assumed that what you consider as acceptable behavior is acceptable to all?

- If you did set boundaries, did you communicate them clearly?

Setting boundaries in relationships like friendships doesn't have to be hard. The following steps will guide you in this quest:

1. Start by setting time aside to attend to your needs, even if your most pressing need is only to have time for self-care.

2. Make it evident that you are only available to your friends at certain times unless it is an emergency. Today, it is so easy to send text messages at any time of day and night, and while you can read these messages, you don't have to engage in conversation right away. Tell your friends that after a certain time, you are only responding when it is an emergency. For sure, you want to be available in their time of need, but only if it is really an emergency situation they are in.

3. Expect this boundary to be resisted. If everyone in your circle is used to the fact that you are always just available when they need you, they won't believe you when you tell them that this won't be the case any longer. Therefore, they will most likely continue to behave as they're used to and that is why you need to change your approach. You've communicated this boundary, and now you need to protect it. If you get

messages in the time you've claimed for yourself, don't respond. You can read it, but you don't have to respond immediately. Respond when you said you'll be available again. You'll probably have to do this several times, but eventually, word will spread that this is the case.

4. Will you lose friends? This is another likelihood, but losing people over the fact that you are claiming time for yourself may very well just be a blessing in disguise. Setting boundaries in friendships has proven itself over and again as an effective way to distinguish between true friends and those who are only around to see how they can benefit from your friendship.

5. A great tip to overcome your weakness around saying no to anyone is to buy yourself some time. You don't have to respond right away. When you find yourself trapped to give an answer and seem to lack the courage to say no, reply with a friendly but firm, "I'll let you know."

6. Share your goals and dreams with your friends. Again, the ones who are truly invested in you as a person will support you in working toward these goals. They'll be the ones who keep you accountable to your own plans, working towards realizing your dreams when you are ready to give up. It may be better to put those who don't support your goals into the category of people you don't really have a capacity for in your life.

It is much better to have a couple of good friends who are authentic in the way they support you than to have many friends who consume your time but offer little in return.

- What are your goals and dreams?

- Have you told your friends about it?

- If not, why not?

- If you did, who did you tell? Why only them? Do you consider them to be better friends as sharing this information brought you closer to them?

BENEFITS OF PERSONAL BOUNDARIES

Initially, it may be hard to set certain boundaries in place, especially in friendships. Nonetheless, as time goes by and people begin to settle in around your boundaries, you'll benefit in numerous ways.

GAIN CLARITY ON YOUR IDENTITY

Setting boundaries demands that you know what your values are, who you are as a friend, and how you deserve to be treated in a friendship. It is how it helps you to gain clarity on your identity. When you know who you are and what you want, it becomes easier to communicate your needs with clarity. Through clear communication, you can avoid unnecessary conflicts.

IT ALLOWS YOU TO PRIORITIZE YOUR WELL-BEING

Boundaries reserve certain times for you to invest in yourself. This may be through having time to do a hobby, exercise, or simply enjoy well-deserved rest. It is how you'll be able to improve your mental, physical, and emotional wellness.

BUILD STRONGER BONDS

Boundaries often serve as a filter separating the truly good friends who have your back from those who are only available during good times. It means that the number of friends you may have left after setting boundaries is most likely going to be less than before. But as you'll have fewer people in your life, you'll have more time to invest in them and build stronger relationships with people you really trust to have around.

- What are the benefits you would like to enjoy from setting boundaries in your friendships?

- List occasions in the past that highlighted your need to set boundaries.

- Phrase the boundaries that will protect you in these areas and prevent similar situations in the future.

- How will you communicate these boundaries within your friendships?

QUICK RECAP

- Lacking personal boundaries will harm your health and wellness but also your relationships and how others perceive you.

- When setting your personal boundaries, you need to start by asking what is hurting you.

- By setting boundaries in friendships, you are protecting your time, needs, dreams, and goals, but you are also establishing a filter to separate your true friends from the ones who are merely around to benefit from you.

- Boundaries in your friendship will benefit your self-esteem, improve the strength of these bonds, and provide you with greater clarity on your identity.

WEEK 6

BOUNDARIES IN ROMANTIC RELATIONSHIPS

Walls keep everybody out. Boundaries teach them where the door is. —Mark Groves

When you are in a relationship, you are part of a larger unit, a unit existing of the combined values, beliefs, dreams, needs, and goals of you and your partner. Therefore, it can be easy to assume that there is no room for boundaries within the parameters of your relationship, but making such an assumption and as result, lacking proper boundaries in place can be detrimental to your overall well-being and to your relationship.

JEFF'S AND JULIE'S STORY

Jeff and Julie have been high school sweethearts who were fortunate enough to be accepted at the same college. After graduation, they set off to the next stage of their lives in the city far away from their small hometown.

Jeff came from a less financially privileged home than Julie and, in a certain way, he has grown accustomed to her family always looking down on him and his family. It didn't bother him as much for he was just interested in Julie and not her family. However, he always thought it was only Julie's family who considered him in that regard, and never did he think Julie saw him in the same manner too.

Once they started college and found themselves in a new crowd, a crowd consisting of students from across the state and no longer their small group of close-knit friends from back home, his perspective switched. It was in the big city that he realized that Julie's remarks toward him would often be quite snarly and even degrading. Whenever he would attempt to say something about it to her, she would simply blow him off telling him that he is imagining things.

Gradually, their relationship became strained. What added to their problems was that they shared an apartment that was way more expensive than what Jeff could afford. Julie *couldn't see herself living in any of the ordinary student apartments*, and while her family funded her part of the rent, he had to pick up a job as a waiter to be able to settle his half. Jeff fell into the trap where he placed his dreams and desires on the back burner while he was working hard to give Julie all she wanted. He did this by getting a part-time job.

While he did everything he could to keep her happy, Julie was enjoying an entirely different kind of student life. She didn't feel the brunt of working hard and studying just to make ends meet. Added to that, she would answer his efforts by criticizing his character and diminishing his efforts and achievements. Julie wasn't a bad person, and she did love Jeff; she was just spoiled and expected Jeff to provide for her similarly to how her parents would.

Despite working at a local bar as a barman, and therefore having much less time to study than Julie, he got better marks than her in their exams. Instead of congratulating him, Julie laughed at him; telling him he sure did a great job of copying someone else's work during the exam without being caught.

Jeff felt trapped and he didn't know how to change things so that his relationship with Julie would become what they both had envisioned for so long. It has also been so long that he has been living to meet Julie's expectations that he lost his identity and became the version of Jeff that Julie liked. He just didn't know how to be any different. Yet, he remains aware of the fact that his studies and self-esteem are suffering, and that he needs to do something to save the situation before he loses himself entirely.

Julie's behavior is causing Jeff to feel unappreciated, undervalued, and like he doesn't have the right to express his feelings, or voice his concerns. Other typical signs that can possibly indicate that you need to establish boundaries in your relationship are:

- poor communication
- constant disagreements
- codependency
- losing your identity
- lack of opportunities to voice your concerns

If these signs stay unaddressed, they can have a detrimental impact on your relationship, but also on your self-esteem and confidence. It is important to remember that, even though your relationship is a unit made up of you and your partner, you are still responsible for taking care of yourself. Any chain is only as strong as its weakest link. Your relationship unit's strength will also depend on how strong each of you is as an individual.

Therefore, it remains your responsibility to take care of your body, feelings, words, actions, attitudes, values, preferences, and dreams as an individual who is part of a larger unit. The only way to do this effectively is by setting boundaries.

- What are the challenges you are facing in your relationship?

- Identify your needs that aren't met by your partner or by being part of this romantic bond.

- What will the situation be like a year from today if you don't take the necessary steps to establish boundaries today?

CONSEQUENCES OF VIOLATING RELATIONSHIP BOUNDARIES

There are several ways how boundary violations can damage your relationship, but for now, let's just consider Jeff's situation.

NEGATIVE IMPACT ON YOUR SELF-ESTEEM

Jeff is doing great at school. He is overexerting himself by working hard to earn an extra income while still doing exceptionally well academically. Yet, Julie fails to acknowledge his effort and success. She would rather accuse him of cheating, and in that manner, leave Jeff's self-esteem shredded. Her lack of trust in him is also enough to make him doubt himself.

It is these and similar comments that are almost leaning themselves toward being allegations that are enough to make you start doubting your own identity.

BURNOUT

Jeff is working as a barman to ensure that he has enough money to pay for their more expensive apartment. He would've been able to get by without having to work as well if they could move to a cheaper one. After all, they are still students and there is no need to live in a fancy place. However, due to the lack of boundaries in their relationship, he feels like he can't express himself honestly to Julie. He can't say no to her, and he continues to say yes when he means the opposite.

Not being able to state what he needs is already one major concern linked to violated boundaries and the lack of boundaries, but now Jeff is also left in a position where he has to over-commit himself, and he is bound to experience burnout too.

TRUST ISSUES

While they were still at school and living in the small town they grew up in, Jeff and Julie knew each other as friends. In fact, as is mostly the case in these small towns, they knew everyone in the town. But now it is all different. Even though they are on the same campus daily, and they share an apartment, Jeff is meeting new people at work, and he is living a life entirely unknown to Julie. She, too, is spending time with new friends while Jeff is at work, and these are people who Jeff doesn't know. Both are lacking a sense of trust in the other and their suspicions often fuel even further arguments in the relationship.

SEVEN GOLDEN RULES FOR RELATIONSHIPS

Rather than being too focused on all that is wrong in your relationship, let's shift our focus onto what the ideal state would be, and what the rules are to establish this state.

Before we do, I want you to think about the following:

- What do you appreciate about your partner?

- What annoys or makes you angry about them or their behavior?

- Have you told them this? If not, why not?

- What would your ideal relationship look like? Would it contain happiness, peace, humor, and contentment?

- What do you need to do to transform your current relationship into this ideal situation?

- So, what do you need to do to ensure the holistic wellness of you and your partner to ensure you have a healthy and strong relationship?

RULE #1: STAY GROUNDED

What do I mean by that? If you've been in a relationship for a very long time—or maybe it hasn't been that long it is just a long time for you—it can be easy to forget how life was before you found this person. It can be easy to forget what life was like when you were still single and all your friends had partners, leaving you all alone with nothing else to do on weekend nights than binge-watching one series after the other.

There was a time when the only thing you truly wanted was to be in a relationship, to have a special someone in your life, and to share your life with that person. Then you met the person. You were smitten and ecstatic all at the same time. It was the best time of your life. And then?

Then you grew used to having that person around, and familiarity breeds contempt. Now, you are no longer smitten, and you've never realized that being in love is a feeling, but loving someone is a verb, a choice you make every day to actively participate in bringing out the best in you both so that your relationship can flourish. You need to stay grounded, to remember where you came from, for then you'll appreciate your partner and this will reflect in your words and actions.

- Do you still appreciate your partner?
- What do you do to show them that you do?
- Does your partner still show you that they appreciate you?
- If not, when will you have a discussion to transform your relationship?
- If it is the case that your partner still appreciates you, how do you show your gratitude towards them?

RULE #2: IT DEMANDS WORK TO MAKE IT WORK

Relationships aren't easy. They can be fun when you both are actively putting in the necessary work, but they sure aren't easy. "Why does it need to be so hard?" I often hear people ask.

Well, what is the alternative? Do you want to live in the misery of an unhappy relationship? Or, would you prefer to be single again? If the latter is the case, then be honest about it to your partner, for if the relationship is not the place where you want to be in your life, you are just wasting their time at your convenience.

Do you think it would be easier when you have someone else in your life? Really? What will make that relationship any different after the newness wears off? No, if you want to stay with your partner, putting in the work for the alternative is always worse.

RULE #3: BE A LITTLE SELFISH

Sure, you need to invest in your relationships and put in the work, but you also need to take care of yourself and your needs. Your partner can't make you happy, and you can't do that for them either. Yes, you can contribute to each other's happiness, but you can't take responsibility for anyone's happiness, or expect someone else to make you happy. Therefore, you need to be selfish at times. Use your boundaries to clear time to invest in yourself and your happiness so that your relationship can be happy.

RULE #4: GAIN CLARITY ON WHAT YOU WANT

Julie wanted a partner who had money. That wasn't Jeff. Not yet, at least. Jeff's character is indicative of him being a hard worker, and he comes across as someone committed to making a success of his life, but he wasn't wealthy yet. However, Julie didn't realize it was what she wanted. It appears that she merely assumed that she wanted Jeff, but Jeff wasn't offering her what her heart was searching for.

RULE #5: ASK QUESTIONS

Don't ever assume that you know what your partner is feeling or thinking. Ask questions, even if you've been together for a long time. People change and evolve, and you need to keep track of how your partner progresses to continue knowing them well. Furthermore, everyone enjoys it if someone shows genuine interest in them.

RULE #6: WHAT CAN YOU DO?

Sometimes the most ordinary or bland objects can make the most amazing images just because of the perspective from which the photographer chose to capture the shot. In life, you also need to change your perspective at times. Stop focusing on all you can't do, every way in which your partner is letting you down, and how they aren't doing things for you, and shift your focus onto all they are doing for you, all you can do, and how they still manage to surprise you at times.

RULE #7: DON'T QUIT

If you are sure your partner is the person you want to spend your life with and that you want to be in this relationship, then don't quit. You may not change your partner, but you can change the way they treat you, or respond to you by changing your approach towards them.

By setting up boundaries in your relationship, you gain control over your happiness and gain clarity on who you are, what you need from your partner, and what kind of partner you're willing to be for them. Now, go out and do these things. When necessary, adjust your boundaries so that they become more effective to ensure that the outcome they deliver is mutually beneficial for that is the ultimate purpose of boundaries, regardless of whether it is at work, in friendships, or in your relationship—boundaries need to ensure a mutually beneficial environment.

JEFF'S AND JULIE'S STORY—PART TWO

Jeff finally had enough of the current situation, but he was sure that he loved Julie. So, he invested time in introspection to gain clarity on what he wanted for his life and for their relationship. He wanted their relationship to be built on a foundation that consisted of accountability, cooperation, honesty, trust, and respect. He knew once they'd achieved that, their relationship would be a space where there was love, happiness, fun, romance, humor, peace, and acceptance.

He considered what changes they would have to make and what boundaries he needed in the relationship that will support his self-esteem, will provide him with enough time to have a balanced life, and to have time to work on his relationship again.

Jeff arranged a romantic evening for them and sat down with Julie, giving them the time to have an open and honest conversation during which he could clearly communicate his needs and boundaries. Julie was open to receiving from Jeff and while she did show some degree of resistance at times, she was willing to cooperate and could even set certain boundaries of her own.

Boundaries create structure and this structure provides direction so that relationships are more secure and can grow. Through boundaries, Jeff and Julie could save their relationship and grow closer to each other.

QUICK RECAP

- Boundaries are often perceived as tools to keep others out of your life, yet what they actually do is to direct others how you want them to enter your life.

- Without this direction, relationships start to struggle with concerns like poor communication, codependency, partners losing their identity, constant disagreement, and lacking the chance to voice their concerns.

- Without the structure of boundaries, relationships are at risk of crumbling and falling apart.

- If there are already boundaries in place, but you or your partner are violating them, you are putting yourselves at risk to experience trust issues, suffer from burnout, and to experience a decline in your self-esteem.

- Follow the seven rules of relationships to establish the necessary boundaries in your relationship to sustain it and help it flourish.

WEEK 7

DEALING WITH ANGER AND DISAPPOINTMENT

If you keep your boundaries, those who are angry at you will have to learn self-control for the first time instead of "other control." —Boundaries

It has been three weeks since Jean and his baby sister, Steffi, had a massive fallout. He is almost 10 years older than her and as she has always been the baby in the family, he would be the one who would have to take care of her. While he mostly enjoyed being her older brother and the one she would run to whenever she needed help, he began to feel over recent years that she is asking him to take care of things that she is perfectly capable of doing herself.

By now, he was almost 35 and had a wife and two little kids who demanded his attention, and he didn't want to go to pick up his sister late at night in town anymore when she had too much to drink. He felt that as she recently turned 25, she is old enough to be more responsible.

Jean has expressed his need for her to be more responsible before, but he never set any boundaries in this regard. Nevertheless, when she phoned him when it was almost midnight about three weeks ago, he was furious. His youngest had the flu and kept them up all night and they just got the little one to sleep when she phoned and woke up the entire home.

Jean jumped in his car, speeding to where his sister said she was and on their way to her apartment, he lost his cool a little, telling her that she is a brat with no consideration for the lives of anyone else. She was drunk and furious when she jumped out of his car, screaming at him that she had had it with him before slamming the door.

Since then, he hasn't heard anything from Steffi and that suited him just fine. If she wants to be angry, she must be, but he is not giving in and reaching out to her first. However, he didn't realize how angry his sister was until it was their dad's birthday and she didn't show up for the celebration.

His mom just told him that Steffi said if he is going to be there, she won't be coming.

This really made him furious because Jean felt that Steffi is now punishing their parents for her inability to look after herself. He phoned her after the family dinner and to his surprise, she answered but only to make it clear to him that she is still livid with him.

Late that night his phone rang and he was caught off guard when he saw it was his mom calling and not Steffi. Jean's mom was so upset she could hardly speak and all he could make out was that Steffi was in an accident and in which hospital she was. He rushed off to see her. She was lucky and sustained minor injuries but she did have a DUI charge against her name and her car was a write-off.

He was relieved to learn that she was going to be okay but still felt so bad that he immediately apologized for their argument. Instead of apologizing as well, Steffi took his guilt and played on that, stating that she wanted to phone him but was too scared he would scream at her again. She said that she is just grateful that she didn't get any serious injuries as she didn't want Jean to live with this guilt all his life.

That night, Jean walked out of the hospital, realizing that it is now more important than ever before that he sets boundaries with his sister. He also knew that he would have to prepare himself not to respond to her anger or guilt trips if he was serious about achieving a mutually beneficial outcome.

THE EMOTIONS THAT ARISE ONCE MET WITH BOUNDARIES

Whether it is in friendship, family, or romantic relationships that you introduce your boundaries, you can be sure that they'll be met with resistance. The most common way people will resist your boundaries is by expressing their anger.

ANGER

When this happens, you may be tempted to give in and let go of your boundaries in the hope that those who resist them will change their behavior automatically, but doing this will be foolish.

Those who react with anger once you set your boundaries are usually quite self-centered people who believe that the world revolves around them and that they are entitled to what it is you are taking away from them with your boundaries. They are people who have much bigger problems to deal with internally and, therefore, you shouldn't take this anger personally. Rather, observe it realistically, because setting these boundaries was perhaps the best thing you did for yourself.

- Have you ever set boundaries and it was met with anger?
- Describe the situation.

- Why do you think the other person responded with anger?

- How did you react?

- Did you give in to their will and demands? If so, did your situation improve at all?

- If not, how is your life better having these boundaries in place?

GUILT

Guilt is another common response to the introduction of boundaries. Steffi tried it on her brother. It is quite common in families and then, of course, also in relationships. Why is guilt such an effective response to prevent boundaries? Simply because most people internalize guilt and store it in their shadow self.

Here, it can fester and gain control over their lives, and unless you are courageous enough to stand in your convictions, you'll most likely let go of your boundaries to escape the pain guilt can cause. You'll only be able to stand firm in your convictions if you have clarity on why you have chosen certain boundaries and what you want to protect by having these boundaries in place.

- What is it that you want to protect with your boundaries?

- Have you thought through the process to be sure that the boundaries you've chosen will be the most effective way to achieve what you desire?

- Are you standing strong in your convictions not to be brought off track by a display of guilt?

WHY DO PEOPLE RESPOND THIS WAY

There are several reasons why your boundaries will be met with anger or guilt. In some cases, it can be simply because the other person is so self-centered that they don't have any real concern about your well-being. But it can also be that they are insecure and may feel rejected by your boundaries. This can be hurtful to them, leaving them feeling lonely and helpless.

Nonetheless, these feelings are still not a reason to let go of your boundaries. You need to be selfish and take care of your needs first. Even if you try your hardest, you aren't *911* and you can't rush to everyone's aid, especially if your cup is empty because you never invest in yourself.

Knowing that your boundaries may upset others can help you to prepare for all possible responses, and it will provide you with empathy when you communicate your boundaries, encouraging you to do so with clarity and by providing reasons for your decision.

TIPS TO HELP YOU OVERCOME THE RESISTANCE

So, now you have expressed your boundaries and unleashed a tonne of emotions. The situation didn't play out at all as you've envisioned and quite frankly, you are starting to wonder if you did the right thing. You did! You have no control over how the other person is going to respond, and your priority remains your own state of wellness. But it is still hard, right? The following tips will help you through this tough phase.

- Realize that your boundaries aren't the problem, nor is the fact that you claim some space for yourself.

- Observe the other person's anger from a realistic perspective. Sure you can see it, but it isn't yours and you don't have to absorb it either.

- Don't let their anger serve as your cue to let go of your boundaries. You've taken the first step and this is the hardest. From here onwards, you only need to remain consistent.

- Make sure that you have a support network you can turn to when things get tough.

- Realize that the other person may want some distance between you and them. It is okay. You don't need to force them to be close to you moving forward. They'll come back to you when they are ready and if they don't, they are not a great fit to be with you anyway.

THREE HELPFUL WAYS TO COMMUNICATE

YOUR BOUNDARIES

Regardless of how hard it is to express your boundaries, never procrastinate on doing so simply because your boundaries will be challenged. Never communicate any boundaries either because you are angry or out of resentment. In these moments, you aren't in control of your emotions and may say things you'll regret later on.

Always keep in mind that the intention of setting boundaries is to put a structure in place in the relationship that will be mutually beneficial. It should support the bond and not leave permanent emotional scars.

When you express your boundaries, be kind and explain your boundaries clearly, assure the other person that you don't want to hurt them by setting these boundaries, and that you are doing it to benefit you both.

The following tips will guide you along the way:

1. **Start by taking small steps.** Whenever you bring change into your life, whether it is to live healthier or to stop being abused by someone you love or care for, take small steps. Small steps will be met with less resistance, and once you see that they are accepted, your courage to introduce larger boundaries will be more and it will be easier for you.

2. **Be consistent in your steps.** That is the second secret to success when working towards transformation. Consistency is vital. This would be

consistent in two regards. You need to be consistent in the fact that the same boundaries are valid for all, and you also need to stick to the same rules when it comes to your boundaries. For example, Jean's boundaries will never be effective if one day he refuses to help his sister and the very next day he gives in. Every time you are going to give in when your boundaries are tested or resisted, you only give the other person hope that they should proceed with their resistance, and eventually, your boundaries will fall away. The more consistent you are in protecting your boundaries, the quicker the resistance will pass.

3. **Be compassionate**. You don't want to hurt the other person, and you know that you are telling them something they may not want to hear, so keep that in mind. You can also soften the blow by asking them what boundaries they would like to put in place to protect their interest. By doing this, you can make them feel like this is not a one-sided attempt to push them away, but much rather a mature, mutual decision to be more responsible with your relationship.

In the end, it is also important to remember that, regardless of how you try to accommodate the other person, and how hard you try to do it in the right manner, you have no control over how the other person will respond. You can only do and think for yourself and have no influence on the other person's actions.

JEAN AND STEFFI TALK AGAIN

After Steffi recovered from her injuries and her legal concerns caused by her drunk driving were sorted out, Jean met up with his sister again. He phoned her up beforehand and scheduled an appointment where the two of them could meet on the mutual ground to discuss the situation.

He explained to his sister that he has different priorities now, and that he has a lot of confidence in her that she is capable of taking care of herself. He stated that he wants to be there for her when she truly needs him, but that she needs to take responsibility for her life too, and that whenever she does, he is immensely proud of his baby sister.

The two could agree under what circumstances and what times she was allowed to reach out to him, and Steffi agreed to take better care of herself. They expressed how much they mean to each other and that they don't want to lose each other. The fear of being left aside was pressing heavily on Steffi as Jean has a family and she had to share him. Yet, he convinced her that he wants her to be part of his family and to play a role in his kids' lives. He wanted her to be the big aunt and to care for them as he cared for her all the time.

QUICK RECAP

- Expect to have your boundaries resisted.

- When you communicate your boundaries, it is quite common for the other person to respond with anger or to make you feel guilty.

- There are several reasons why people have this response, varying from them being self-centered and only keen to get what they can from you to them feeling rejected, pushed away, or even lonely.

- Consider the other person's emotions when you break the news and be sure to pick a suitable time and place to do so.

- Never reveal your boundaries while being angry or resentful.

- Take small steps, be consistent, and show compassion for the other person.

- Remember that boundaries are intended to provide structure to let your relationship grow and it should be mutually beneficial.

- Even if you have done all you could to ease into your boundaries, accept that you have no control over what the other person thinks or feels, or how they'll respond. You need to take care of your well-being.

WEEK 8

DEALING WITH YOUR UNLEASHED EMOTIONS

If someone thinks you're being dramatic or selfish, then they obviously haven't walked a mile in your shoes. It's not important for you to explain yourself. You get a pass here. Don't let anyone else try to saddle you with guilt or shame. If you need your space, take it. —Unknown

In the previous chapter, we've touched on why people get upset when you set your boundaries. However, even when you're so well-prepared to deal with the emotional response of others when you set boundaries, you can forget to prepare yourself for all the emotions you may feel when you do.

It is also important to note that setting boundaries is one thing and probably the easiest part of the process. Communicating your boundaries for the very first time is something completely different and much harder. Then, there is also the third stage of the process: protecting your boundaries. This is when you'll realize that setting boundaries is never a once-off task. No, it is an ongoing process.

BOUNDARY SETTING WILL UNLEASH EMOTIONS

How hard or easy it will be for you to set boundaries will depend entirely on your personality and the level of exposure you've had to boundaries while growing up. In some homes, parents raise their kids with strong boundaries and encourage them to set boundaries of their own. But the odds are also quite high that you don't have any reference of what boundary setting looks like and then it can be an emotional venture.

Another contributing factor to how intense boundary setting will be for you is what your beliefs around boundaries are. If you consider boundaries to be a positive step in a good direction to establish a healthy relationship, then you'll likely enjoy the more emotional calm. But if you consider boundaries in a negative light and are merely turning to them as your last resort as you simply can't handle your current situation anymore, then you may feel a certain degree of internal friction, which can cause you to have an emotional outburst.

- How much exposure have you had to boundaries in the past?

- Do you consider boundaries to be helpful aids to sustain healthy relationships, or are you more negatively inclined when it comes to boundaries?

- What motivated you to set the boundaries you are about to communicate?

However, even when you have had a lot of exposure to boundaries, it may still be hard for you to express yours for no other reason than that they make you feel bad about yourself.

THE LANGUAGE IS SOMETIMES HARSH

Boundary-setting language can at times be very harsh, or you may perceive it to be harsh. While you may have complete clarity on why you need to set these boundaries and you've already gained clarity on why they'll be good for your relationship, you may be catching the other person off-guard.

Added to that is the fact that communication can be tricky. How would you know that the other person is still listening to your reasoning behind your boundaries or why you think it would be good for you both? You just don't, and if you think that they won't listen, you are most probably right. People in general aren't great listeners. Sure, we hear the speaker, but our minds may already be so busy composing a proper response that more than half of the message communicated to us just gets lost.

YOU HAVE NO CONTROL OVER THE OTHER PERSON'S THOUGHTS

Maybe you've worked out an entire plan on how you are going to break the news in small steps, you've picked a great time to share your news, and you've found the perfect setting to do it in. Couple it with preparing your message to convey your boundaries with clarity and you should be good to go, right? No. You have no control over what is happening in the other person's mind, what emotional triggers you may alert, or how well they'll listen to anything you say after opening with a statement like, "We need to talk," which is globally the way to start a serious conversation that will most likely not end well for at least one participant.

There is just nothing much you can do about that. You can give the other person space to calm down and be open to taking up the conversation again when they are ready, but you can't control how it will play out at all.

RESPECT THEIR EMOTIONS BUT DON'T GIVE IN

So, what am I saying to you? That you will very well feel like you've hurt the other person. You may feel ashamed for even suggesting your boundaries or even kind of worthless for needing boundaries. In certain scenarios, it is even possible to feel like an imposter.

While these are all bad feelings to have, expect that these emotions will surface and plan ahead how you'll be dealing with them afterward, rather than finding yourself in the middle of the conversation trapped in a panic because you didn't expect to feel this way. Then, the likelihood of you backtracking on all your well-thought-through plans will only make your next attempt much harder.

Understanding the dynamics of such a conversation is one step you can take to help you deal with the emotional surge in advance. Another is to change your language to be friendlier and accommodating, yet stern. You don't want to hurt anyone, but as you need to protect yourself and you've invested enough time thinking about your options and reasons for taking this step, you have to remain true to your convictions.

But, there are also several steps you can take afterward to ease the pain you may feel and to find certainty in the confusion.

TAMMY'S STORY

Tammy has always been very close to her parents and loves having them around. They stay only a few streets away from them and she'll see them often. However, after the birth of her firstborn, she realized that she and her husband needed a little more space to settle in as a family. However, the greater their need to have some time on their own became, the more often their parents would be around, taking all the time they can get with their grandchild.

The situation began to cause friction between her and her husband, and she knew that she would have to set boundaries with her parents. She understood why they were there all the time, and she also believed that if she aired her concerns, they would understand her reasons.

She waited for the right time and visited them at their home, leaving her baby at home with her husband. She then explained to them that they can't come so often, and even stated when it would be a good time for them to be around. She explained that they needed time together as a family like they also did when they were young parents.

Tammy tried her best to explain her reasons to her parents, but she could see that she triggered an emotional response in her mom, who soon stormed out after mumbling something.

Tammy felt so bad. She left their home guilt-ridden, feeling like she was a terribly ungrateful daughter. After all, that was what her mom implied before she ran out. She did what she could, but also understood that she had no control over their behavior. All she could do now was to give them the space they needed to process what she told them.

It took them four days before they phoned to make an appointment to see their grandchild. Tammy could feel that there was a bit of childish sarcasm in their behavior but decided not to say anything about it. Her parents' first visit was quite stiff, but from there onwards, it became better. Sure, her parents tried to push the boundaries, showing up at her home with all kinds of excuses, but she stuck to her convictions. Gradually, the situation improved and all were happy once again.

OVERCOMING FEELINGS OF GUILT

How did Tammy overcome her feelings of guilt? The following steps will help.

JOURNALING

She started journaling daily. In her journal, she could let go of her emotional burden without upsetting anyone in the process. Here, she would be authentic about how she felt and even managed to change her perspective of matters to be sure that she handled the matter correctly. It was how she could process all her negative feelings until they were finally gone.

SUPPORT NETWORK

She also reached out to a couple of friends who served as her support network. Getting insights from others on her situation helped her find peace with her choices. It also helped to know that some of the ladies in her network went through the same thing with their parents and it worked out fine.

By confronting these emotions in her journal and through the many conversations she had, she processed her feelings and could so unburden herself.

- What negative feelings are resting heavily on you right now after communicating your boundaries?

- Are you perhaps holding back on stating what you want because you are scared that you'll feel bad afterward?

The only way to gain is through pain, but if you avoid the pain, there will only be more that remains.

WHAT DO YOU NEED TO DO RIGHT NOW?

- Are you about to communicate a boundary?

- Are you perhaps procrastinating on doing it simply because you don't want to experience the surge of emotions?

Decide in advance what it is you want to feel after you've communicated your boundaries. Maybe you would want to feel relief that you've taken the first step in the right direction. Or, it can be that you want to feel pride for standing up, possibly for the first time ever, for what is important to you.

After having such a conversation, you are likely going to feel mixed emotions. However, the ones you are going to focus on are the ones that will feel the most prominent to you. So, decide in advance what feelings you are going to focus on to make this entire conversation less daunting.

QUICK RECAP

- Expressing your boundaries is going to cause a surge of emotions in the other person. You are expecting this to happen, but you can be caught off guard by the emotions triggered in you when you have this chat.

- How easy or hard it will be for you to state how you are feeling will depend on the level of exposure you've had to set boundaries in the past, and how well these worked out. Your personality will also influence your feelings.

- While setting boundaries can be hard, you can prepare yourself mentally for it in advance.

- Expect to feel guilty, ashamed, or even needy to put these boundaries in place.

- However, stay true to your beliefs, values, and convictions.

- Be kind in the language you use but know that a lot of what you say may not even be heard.

- Give the other person space to process what you've said.

- Journal about your feelings to unburden yourself of this weight.

- Reach out to your network to gain support and new perspectives from them.

WEEK 9

EFFECTIVE WAYS TO COMMUNICATE YOUR BOUNDARIES

Honoring your own boundaries is the clearest message to others to honor them, too. —Gina Greenlee

During the first couple of years of our lives, we learn to speak, and for the rest of our lives, we learn how to master the art of proper communication. Why is learning how to communicate effectively a lifelong task? Well, communicating effectively, or in other words, talking in a way that others would listen and listening so that others are keen to express themselves with greater clarity, is a form of art.

Communication is a complex combination of elements relying on words, but also on non-verbal elements like tone, body language, gestures, and non-verbal sounds. Effective communication is a requirement in most circumstances in life and is especially of extreme importance during those sensitive moments when the entire existence of a relationship depends on it. One of those moments is when you express your boundaries.

COMMUNICATING YOUR BOUNDARIES—AN ART

Like with any other form of art, communication too requires a lot of practice and patience to get it right. Even once you've familiarized yourself with all the tips and techniques I am sharing with you in this chapter, you'll still have to spend some time practicing them before you'll become a master in communication. One of the reasons why it is such a challenge is because there are several aspects you need to consider, and the other is, of course, that you want to apply all the elements of effective communication naturally in your conversation.

That said, keep in mind that, even after a lot of practice and showing yourself as a master of communication, the conversation in which you express your boundaries may still not run as smoothly as you've envisioned simply because there are several aspects to such a conversation that are just beyond your control.

- You are touching on a sensitive topic that might trigger the other person

- You have no idea how they'll respond

- You may not have complete control over the setting

- You don't know what the other person might say that can trigger an emotional response in you.

I am not saying this to make it even harder for you to approach such a challenging conversation. No, I am saying this so that you understand before the conversation takes place that, even if it doesn't go the way you've envisioned, taking the first step remains vital. Regardless of how well the conversation went, you'll break the ice, and from there onwards, expanding on your boundaries, reaffirming them, and explaining why you've chosen to employ them only becomes easier, as it is merely a repetition and expansion of what was already said.

Repetition is of course another important aspect to keep in consideration as it is undeniably part of expressing, establishing, and maintaining your boundaries.

BE FIRM, BUT GENTLE

When communicating your boundaries, the primary purpose remains to express your boundaries with such clarity that they are easily understood. This goes hand-in-hand with your intention to effectively stop certain behavior patterns of the other person and this is something you can only establish if you manage to arouse a positive reaction in the other person, may this person be a parent, friend, coworker, or romantic partner.

You want to come across as serious regarding the matter you are addressing and, therefore, you need to be firm, but you also want to be kind and avoid having them feel like they are under attack, and that is why you need to be gentle.

It is often not as much the boundaries themselves, the wording thereof, or even what exactly it stipulates that brings about results, but the fact that you are expressing them toward the other person. As this is where the initial impact of boundaries is nestled, you have to keep in consideration that stating your boundaries can easily make the other person feel rejected or even considered to be worthless by your boundaries.

See? There is a very fine line between applying enough assertiveness while remaining gentle and understanding, and finding the balance between applying enough assertion and being gentle enough is truly challenging. Yet, you have to start somewhere, and the best place to do this is by starting with the basics.

THE PRINCIPLES OF ASSERTIVE COMMUNICATION

Effective communication consists of far more than merely the eloquent use of words, so you should also expect that assertive communication demands far more than merely using words. Before we get to the principles though, let's quickly stop and pause at the concept of assertive communication and what exactly it means. Here, a good starting point is to state what it doesn't mean.

Assertive communication is not supposed to be confrontational. It should be effective, and it should come across that you are demanding respect for your rights and opinions. The way you do this can be described as elegant, honest, and transparent, and the primary purpose of assertive communication is always to reduce friction and conflict in the long term while it will likely ruffle some feathers in the immediate conversation.

THE NON-VERBAL ELEMENTS OF EFFECTIVE COMMUNICATION

These parts often make up most of the conversation.

EYE CONTACT

One of the most basic ways to come across as assertive is through eye contact. By making and holding eye contact with the other person, you are making it evident that you aren't intimidated by the situation or by having to address the matter with them. It shows how serious you are, and by making eye contact, you can already remove some misconceptions linked to your intentions for having the conversation.

BODY LANGUAGE

Another non-verbal cue indicating your seriousness toward the matter is your body language. By holding a pose or stance that is upright and radiates confidence and strength, you are already expressing your assertiveness while you haven't even said one word yet.

FACIAL EXPRESSIONS

Facial expressions should be pretty neutral. You don't want to look angry, but also not like you are taking this matter lightheartedly. Thus, a neutral expression might be best. It will show the other person that you aren't taking the matter lightly, but also that you aren't shutting them out entirely.

TIMING

Timing is another aspect to consider. There is a time and place for everything, and you need to choose your timing wisely, keeping in mind how this will influence the success of this quest.

VERBAL ELEMENTS

This is not the time to express blame or resentment, nor would you want to come across as threatening. Your words should reflect that there are consequences if your boundaries aren't respected, but you don't want it to sound threatening as this will only trigger defensiveness, and even hostility, in the other person.

Clarity is often rooted in simplicity. Therefore, don't overdo it with coloring in your words. You want to communicate a clear and direct message using fewer words rather than confuse the other person with lengthy explanations and expressions.

Use positive language instead of using this conversation as an opportunity to criticize the other person for what they've done or their repeated behavior.

PREPARE FOR RESISTANCE

You can be sure that there will be resistance, and entering into such a conversation knowing that your boundaries will be resisted is already half of your battle won. The other half can be won by familiarizing yourself with the reasons why people resist your boundaries and how they'll do it.

RESISTANCE THROUGH CONTROL

The other person may resist what you are saying by trying to take control of the conversation. If this is the case, the other person may likely come across as angry and show either verbal or physical aggression toward you. In case you are met by a display of physical aggression, it is best to remove yourself from the situation as soon as possible.

However, their approach can also be less direct and they may try to sway your mind and so control your thoughts. An example of this would be a statement like, "I hear what you are saying, but don't you think your perception of my behavior is exaggerated?" A question structured like this is not to show you that they are actually listening to what you are saying, but to put some doubt in your mind about whether you aren't perhaps the wrong one.

RESISTANCE THROUGH INTIMIDATION

Here you can come across a range of different responses like gaslighting, shaming, arguing, or even diminishing your needs and wishes. They'll try to sway the conversation to the point where you come across as the one who is causing all the problems, that your perception of events is merely your imagination, and that you are unreasonable for setting boundaries and the way you are doing it.

RESISTANCE THROUGH GUILT

For the longest time, this person you are addressing has gotten away with access to your life, what you have to offer, and your time without any boundaries. While they should be feeling guilty for taking from the relationship without making an equal investment of their resources, they'll try to make you feel guilty for taking away their free access to your life. In this case, you may hear statements insinuating that you are selfish.

HOW TO RESPOND?

Understand that when you are expressing your boundaries, it is not a case of whether you'll be confronted by one—or more—of the above reactions, but rather when you are confronted. I still have to come across a situation where boundaries were communicated and there was no resistance.

- Keep in mind that the angry person is usually the one who is in the wrong.

- Yes, they may be angry or upset over what you've said, but that doesn't make it any less true.

- It is their anger you are facing and you don't have to claim it. Choose to not allow the fact that they are portraying a strong emotional response to upset you back.

- If the situation becomes too heated, rather take a break and continue the conversation later on.

- Don't fall for guilt. Guilt is essentially only a disguise to hide anger or insecurities.

SAMPLE PHRASES TO OVERCOME RESISTANCE

There are many ways you can express yourself or respond to resistance during these tough conversations. I am sharing several examples to offer you guidance in this regard.

RESPONSES WHEN YOU DISAGREE

- I find your approach interesting, but I am not convinced that it will work or that it is realistic.

- I value your time and appreciate the fact that you were willing to listen to what I had to say, but I am sticking to my convictions, and attempts to change my mind will be a waste of time.

- I disagree with your perspective. Would you mind explaining your reasoning behind your viewpoint?

RESPONSES WHEN THE OTHER PERSON TRIES TO WEAR YOU DOWN

- I think this conversation was loaded with information, and it would be best for us to take some time to digest what was said before we continue further at a later stage.

- I find your response surprising and it is a lot to take in at once. I'll need some time to think it over, and I suggest that we continue this conversation later on.

- I am not willing to engage in this conversation any longer. Let's step back for a while to give it all some thought and then we can return with a fresh approach to the matter.

RESPONSES WHEN THE OTHER PERSON TRIES TO STIR EMOTIONS

- I can see that this is upsetting to you, so I suggest that we take a break so that you can compose yourself.

- I respect your feelings, but I am confident in my decision.

- My reasons are personal and I don't expect you to understand them.

While not every pre-composed response may be relevant to your unique situation when you have such a conversation, these examples do serve as inspiration to compose your own responses, and having some structured responses on hand will leave you feeling more empowered to have this conversation and give you direction when you need it.

- Are you preparing for a conversation to express your boundaries?

- What type of resistance do you expect?

- Start phrasing some suitable responses for this resistance.

QUICK RECAP

- Talking is easy, but effective communication is a form of art mastered only through patience and practice.

- Effective communication consists of a small verbal element and a much larger non-verbal part, which refers to gestures, body language, tone, and non-verbal sounds.

- Be gentle but firm when expressing your boundaries.

- Rely on all the elements of communication when you engage in assertive communication to express your boundaries.

- Always expect resistance.

WEEK 10

SEVEN GOLDEN RULES TO BETTER SELF-CARE

At first, you will probably feel selfish, guilty, or embarrassed when you set a boundary. Do it anyway and tell yourself you have a right to self-care. Setting boundaries takes practice and determination, don't let anxiety or low self-esteem prevent you from taking care of yourself. —Terri Cole

If setting boundaries is so hard and places so much strain on you, why do you want to do it? Sure, by now you know that you need to express your boundaries with clarity, but before you can do that, you also need to have clarity in your own mind regarding why you want to bring these boundaries into your life.

In this chapter, you'll learn that boundary setting is a form of self-care. It is only one of several ways to take care of yourself—as we'll explore in this chapter—but is it a method without which self-care won't be possible at all?

SELF-CARE THROUGH BOUNDARIES

There may be many reasons why you want to set up certain boundaries, but, ultimately, there is only one reason that explains all boundaries ever set, regardless of whether it is personal or professional, boundaries with family, friends, or romantic partners. This reason is that you want to improve the quality of your life.

Yes, setting boundaries is a form of self-care, a way to protect your physical, mental, and emotional health to ensure a life reflecting happiness, contentment, confidence, fun, growth, and anything else you would like in your life now and in the future. When you set boundaries, you are stating that you've identified your needs and are doing what is necessary to answer these needs.

Furthermore, through boundaries you apply effective stress management, take care of the state of your relationships, and claim a percentage of your time to invest in yourself, may it be to do a hobby, for exercise, self-reflection, or just to relax.

It doesn't matter, as long as it helps you to maintain a balanced lifestyle.

- What do you need right now?

- Spend some time exploring which of your needs aren't cared for at the moment or what areas in your life demand your attention right away. Maybe it is a relationship with a loved one that is on shaky grounds, or perhaps you're exhausted and need to reclaim some of your time to recuperate.

- Now, identify what boundaries you need to set up to answer these needs.

- Rely on the knowledge you've gained to see this venture through.

SELF-CARE BY PRACTICING MINDFULNESS

What is mindfulness and how will it help you? Mindfulness refers to a state of mind where you remain mentally present in the moment. It requires an active effort to become more aware of your feelings, thoughts, sensations, and experiences in the present. This awareness of the now is at the core of mindfulness, and secondary to that is to consider everything you are aware of with a gentle acceptance. Mindfulness is not about judging any of the things you are aware of, but just acknowledging what you are aware of.

Are you ready to practice mindfulness right now?

MINDFULNESS EXERCISE #1: BODY SCAN

1. Find a spot where you can sit undisturbed for five minutes. Choose a relatively quiet spot.

2. Set a timer for five minutes so that you can focus on the exercise and not on the time.

3. Close your eyes and make yourself comfortable. You can lie down on your back or maintain a comfortable seated position.

4. Inhale deeply, hold your breath for about four counts, and exhale slowly and deliberately. Repeat this breathing about five times.

5. Shift your focus to your toes. Stretch them, wiggle them, and become aware of any feeling, sensations, discomfort, or even pain in them.

6. Move onto your feet and do the same. Always stretch and relax your muscles, and take note of any sensations you feel in the specific area.

7. Work your way to your ankles, calves, knees, thighs, buttocks, and then first your lower back before moving to your upper back.

8. Stretch your fingers, then move onto your hands, wrists, lower arm muscles, upper arm muscles, and then your shoulder and neck area.

9. Pull your face, wiggle your nose, and relax. Once you reach the crown of your head and scan your entire body, breathe a couple of times deeply again, focusing on how the air passes through your nose and into your lungs, and out again.

10. Now open your eyes.

MINDFULNESS EXERCISE #2: OBSERVATION AND AWARENESS

The previous exercise helps you become aware of your body and internal sensations, and this exercise will help you gain awareness of your external environment.

1. You can choose your location. It can be a park, or at a street café.

2. Find your position and breathe deeply a couple of times to center your thoughts and focus.

3. Next, use your senses to gather information about your environment.

4. Take note of what you see, identify any scents in the air, and what sounds you hear.

    a. Do you feel a little breeze on your cheeks? Do you smell freshly baked bread coming from an oven, or perhaps you can immerse yourself in the scent of a plant flowering nearby?

    b. Are you eating something? What does it taste like? What is the texture like?

Mindfulness simply requires that you become more aware of your current environment, how it makes you feel, and what sensations it triggers, but also how you feel and what you are experiencing internally. It is easy to practice even while taking care of ordinary tasks.

For example, the next time you're doing the dishes, take note of the citrus scent of the dishwashing liquid, the sensation of warm water, and the slippery feeling of the water, rather than merely rushing through the task while your mind is stressing over future events.

SELF-CARE THROUGH BUILDING YOUR SELF-ESTEEM

Every task and suggestion I've listed in this chapter will make a positive contribution to your self-esteem. But these steps are only some of the methods you can employ to improve your self-esteem, will better your relationships, improve your holistic health and wellness, and help you have a more positive and daring outlook on life.

A few more tips to help you to grow your self-esteem even stronger are:

- Stop comparing yourself to anyone but the person you were yesterday. Only compete against yourself as nobody is exactly like you, and comparing or competing against anyone but yourself is both futile and draining.

- Make positive affirmations part of your daily routine. Write positive notes to yourself and leave them up on your bathroom mirror, the fridge door, or your computer screen. Look at yourself in the mirror and say these affirmations out loud. For example, "I am strong and resourceful," or "I am much loved and appreciated."

- Be kind to yourself. Why is it so much easier to be kind to others than yourself? Why is it that you'll be much harsher in what you say to yourself than to others? Is it perhaps because we tend to be nicer to those whose eyes we can look at?

BUILD YOUR SELF-ESTEEM BY BEING KIND TO YOURSELF

I want to share a quick, but very powerful exercise with you. It won't take much longer than five minutes, but it usually leaves a lasting impression.

- Go to a mirror, set a timer for five minutes, and look at your reflection in the mirror.

- Just look at your face and into your eyes. Observe, don't judge—Now is not the time to notice any new wrinkles or gray hair. Just see them, acknowledge their existence, and move on.

- Then shift your focus to your eyes. Stare deeply into your eyes and think about the dreams, hopes, fears, strengths, and insecurities behind those eyes; your eyes. Think about the fact that those eyes belong to a person who also deserves kindness, appreciation, to matter, and to belong.

- Take a moment of self-awareness to identify any new emotions you may feel. Do you feel sad looking into your own eyes? Perhaps you are feeling guilty because you know how hard you can be at times on the person behind these eyes.

It doesn't matter. What matters is that you take this opportunity to remind yourself that you, too, deserve your kindness and care.

SELF-CARE THROUGH FITNESS

A healthy body hosts a healthy mind and feel-good emotions. People are complex beings with several parts of our existence that all work together to enjoy optimal health. Your emotional health plays in on your mental and physical health while the opposite is also the case.

Thus, if you want to enjoy optimal health, it is important to include exercise as part of a healthy lifestyle in your self-care routine.

- Exercise improves longevity and overall wellness as it strengthens your muscles and bones. It is a way to get rid of excess weight and sustain mobility.

- It is a form of relaxation and plays a vital role in stress management, helping you to take care of your mental health.

- Exercise also increases the release of feel-good hormones, like serotonin, that uplift your mood, and so take care of your emotional wellness.

Even a brisk walk around the block or in your local park will count as exercise and a great place to start to care for yourself in this regard.

- What types of exercise do you prefer?

- How much time do you have to spend on exercise?

- What is your fitness level at the moment?

- If you haven't been exercising for a while, what can you start doing right now to take care of yourself?

SELF-CARE IN NATURE

Spending time in nature can easily be combined with exercise. For example, let's say you take a brisk walk in your local park. Then you've given your body a workout and can reap all the benefits resulting from that, but you've also spent time in the relaxing environment nature offers.

The colors, sounds, and scents you find in nature are all naturally calming and uplift the mood.

- What is your favorite outdoor activity? Do you like going to the beach, mountains, or just the park?

- Identify a natural environment close to your home where you would like to spend more time.

While exercising in nature is a wonderful way to take care of yourself, you can also choose to just sit and enjoy your surroundings, or even meditate in nature.

SELF-CARE THROUGH ALONE TIME

When was the last time you spoiled yourself? Spending time with yourself, especially doing something you like, and spoiling yourself a little is a huge investment in self-care. These alone moments, whether it is having a coffee while reading a book at your local coffee shop, or browsing at your farmer's market, are time spent getting to know yourself better. It is a time during which you get to learn how to appreciate yourself and how to just be authentically you.

- When last did you schedule a date with yourself?
- Set a date right now for when you'll be going somewhere on your own.
    - ☐ Where will you be going?
    - ☐ What will you do?
    - ☐ How often can you fit in these dates?

SELF-CARE THROUGH SOCIAL CONNECTIONS

Having boundaries in place doesn't mean that you are isolating yourself from loved ones and friends. No, let me remind you that boundaries aren't supposed to keep people out, it just directs them on when and how they are allowed into your life. Having boundaries in place that are mutually respected is even something that can bring you and your loved ones closer to each other as it becomes a bond of intimacy.

There are several benefits you can enjoy from your social connections. Some of these are:

- a healthy self-esteem
- declining stress and anxiety levels
- lower risks of depression and symptoms of depression can improve due to these connections
- more empathy toward others
- an increased sense of purpose
- you feel a sense of belonging
- it even boosts your immune system.

Therefore, expanding and maintaining your network of social connections surely is a form of self-care.

Even if you aren't by nature an outgoing person, or perhaps you are more introverted and finding it difficult to meet new people, there are still many ways you can expand your circle of friends.

- Join groups with a shared interest, like a gardening or book club.

- Volunteering is another way for you to meet like-minded people.

- Get involved in your community.

- Push yourself a little by taking some risks, this will help you overcome the fear of reaching out to strangers.

You can meet people, strengthen your connection, and set up boundaries to protect your interest all at the same time.

QUICK RECAP

- Ultimately, the reason why you are pursuing boundaries and putting yourself through the challenges of setting them up and communicating them to others is to improve your quality of life.

- Setting boundaries is a great way to take care of yourself, but it is not the only way to do it.

- You can also practice self-care by practicing mindfulness, working on your self-esteem, exercising, spending time in nature, spending time in your own company, and expanding your social connections.

- Proper self-care helps you take great care of yourself to ensure optimal, lasting mental, physical, and emotional health.

CONCLUSION

You get what you tolerate. —Henry Cloud

There are an endless number of reasons why you may feel the need to set boundaries in your life. Maybe you've identified straight away with Sandy's inability to stop agreeing to do everything, or perhaps it was only later on that you felt Calvin's frustration with his needy mother. Perhaps you are finding yourself in a similar relationship situation as Jeff and Julie, and are desperately hoping for the same improvement they've managed.

All of these reasons simply boil down to one thing: you want to improve the quality of your life. You want to feel happier, healthier, more content, and live a more balanced life, and any reason to desire such a change is valued and justifies the discomfort of setting boundaries.

Throughout, we've covered every detail related to setting boundaries, why you need boundaries, what happens to you mentally if your boundaries are violated, and the consequences of life without any boundaries. We explored how they contribute to your life, and how you should go about setting personal boundaries, but also setting up boundaries in your friendships and romantic relationships.

Then, we also shifted our perspective to understand the feelings and responses of the other person, why they may be upset, and how they're likely to react so that you can enter into such a conversation well-prepared and with sufficient confidence.

An important contributing factor to the success of your boundaries is how well you communicate them, so we stood still here for quite a while too. In addition, we explored six more steps you can take to improve your quality of life.

From all of this information, I want to highlight two points as these capture the entire essence of boundaries for me.

- The purpose of boundaries is not to manipulate others but to ensure a mutually beneficial situation for all.

- Boundaries aren't intended to block people out of your life but to direct them on how and when they are allowed into your life.

Armed with this knowledge, you are prepared to set up effective and beneficial boundaries, boundaries that add structure to ensure progress, and boundaries that will support the intimacy in your relationships rather than create distance. You have all the instruments in your communication toolbox to enter into the conversation regarding your boundaries with confidence, use this knowledge to your advantage, and achieve your goal—the goal of improving your quality of life.

Next, you need to place every aspect and relationship in your life under the microscope to see where you can make minor adjustments to enjoy immense prosperity and joy.

Now that you are familiar with boundaries and how they can benefit you, how much longer do you want to wait and place those things you treasure at risk before getting your boundaries in place?

SCAN THE QR CODE TO LEAVE YOUR HONEST REVIEW ON AMAZON

If this material was helpful to you, I would be very grateful to you if you will share it with your friends or with someone you know who needs it.

Also, in order for me to improve things in the future, you can share your honest opinion by leaving a sincere review on Amazon. It truly means a lot to me :)

Simply scan this QR code to do just that!

OTHER BOOKS WRITTEN BY ANDREI NEDELCU

<u>Facing and Overcoming Codependency: Practical Guidance to Fix Your Codependency, Stop Being a People Pleaser, and Start Loving Yourself</u>

Scan the QR code to check it out

Facing and Overcoming Codependency: From Being Needy & Clingy to Having Amazing, Authentic, and Loving Relationships

Scan the QR code to check it out

The Only Cognitive Behavioral Therapy Book You'll Ever Need: 2022 Life-Changing CBT Strategies to Overcome Depression, Anxiety, Insomnia, Intrusive Thoughts, and Anger

Scan the QR code to check it out

REFERENCES

Beeslaar, E. (2019, April 16). *Healthy vs. unhealthy boundaries.* Healthy Relationships Initiative. https://healthyrelationshipsinitiative.org/healthy-vs-unhealthy-boundaries/

Bestquotes. (n.d.). *70+ Motivational Setting boundaries quotes to set the importance of relationships.* Terse Sayings. https://tersesayings.com/setting-boundaries-quotes/

Better health channel. (n.d.). *Strong relationships, strong health.* Better Health.

https://www.betterhealth.vic.gov.au/health/HealthyLiving/Strong-relationships-strong-health

Bohlin, S. (n.d.). *7. Resistance to boundaries*. Bible.org. https://bible.org/seriespage/7-resistance-boundaries

Boundaries quotes. (n.d.). Picture Quotes. http://www.picturequotes.com/boundaries-quotes

Darcy, A. M. (2019, June 25). *12 Signs you lack healthy boundaries (and why you need them) - Harley Therapy™ Blog*. Harley Therapy™ Blog. https://www.harleytherapy.co.uk/counselling/healthy-boundaries.htm

Degges-White, S. (2021, November 18). *10 Ways that better boundaries can improve your life*. Psychology Today. https://www.psychologytoday.com/za/blog/lifetime-connections/202111/10-ways-better-boundaries-can-improve-your-life

Durvasula, D. R. (2022, July 12). *9 Signs of poor boundaries (and what to do instead)*. MedCircle. https://medcircle.com/articles/signs-of-poor-boundaries/

Eatough, E. (2021, June 30). *Setting boundaries at work and in relationships: A how-to guide.* BetterUp. https://www.betterup.com/blog/setting-boundaries#:~:text=They%20aren

Gilles, G. (n.d.). *The importance of boundaries in romantic relationships.* Mental Help.net. https://www.mentalhelp.net/blogs/the-importance-of-boundaries-in-romantic-relationships/#:~:text=Boundaries%20define%20ownership%20and%20responsibility&text=In%20a%20romantic%20relationship%2C%20the

Gilman, S. (n.d.). *Notice what you choose. Get your free boundary tips weekly by email. Boundaries, #boundaries | Great quotes, Words, Marriage and family therapist.* Pinterest. https://za.pinterest.com/pin/12736811431579041/

Hailey, L. (n.d.). *How to set boundaries: 5 Ways to draw the line politely.* Science of People. https://www.scienceofpeople.com/how-to-set-boundaries/#:~:text=Ways%20to%20Set%20Bounda

ries%20with%20Friends%3A&text=Clearly%20expres s%20when%20you%20feel

Hale Brockway, L. (2021, December 30). *59 phrases to help you set boundaries.* PR Daily. https://www.prdaily.com/59-phrases-to-help-you-set-boundaries/#:~:text=I

Hilton Andersen, C. (2021, May 16). *16 Quotes about boundaries that will help you say "no."* The Healthy. https://www.thehealthy.com/mental-health/boundaries-quotes/

Hogan, M. (n.d.). *Real ones respect boundaries.* Move Me Quotes. https://movemequotes.com/real-ones-respect-boundaries/

How to handle those who get angry at your boundaries. (2020, April 14). Boundaries. https://www.boundaries.me/blog/how-to-handle-those-who-get-angry-at-your-boundaries#:~:text=People%20who%20get%20angry %20at

Lee, K. (2018, September 11). *Why is it so hard to set boundaries?* Psychology Today. https://www.psychologytoday.com/za/blog/rethink-your-way-the-good-life/201809/why-is-it-so-hard-set-boundaries

Lonczak, H. (2020, September 3). *What is assertive communication? 10 Real-life examples.* Positive Psychology. https://positivepsychology.com/assertive-communication/

Manson, M. (n.d.). *The guide to strong relationship boundaries.* Mark Manson. https://markmanson.net/boundaries#boundary-issues

Martin, S. (2016, May 22). *10 Steps to setting healthy boundaries.* Psych Central. https://psychcentral.com/blog/imperfect/2016/05/10-steps-to-setting-healthy-boundaries#10-Steps-to-Setting-Boundaries:

Martin, S. (2019, June 28). *5 Tips for setting boundaries (without feeling guilty)*. Psych Central. https://psychcentral.com/blog/imperfect/2019/06/5-tips-for-setting-boundaries-without-feeling-guilty

Mas, S. (2023, March 20). *4 Examples of boundary violations*. The Truly Charming. https://thetrulycharming.com/examples-of-boundary-violations/

Nicole, A. (2019, August 22). *3 Kind, simple & effective ways to communicate your boundaries*. Medium. https://headway.ginger.io/3-kind-simple-effective-ways-to-communicate-your-boundaries-46dad0989e79

Nitka, D. (2017, May 16). *The importance of setting boundaries*. Connecte Psychology. https://connectepsychology.com/en/2017/05/16/the-importance-of-setting-boundaries/#:~:text=So%20what%20are%20boundaries%3F

Pattemore, C. (2021, June 3). *10 Ways to build and preserve better boundaries.* Psych Central. https://psychcentral.com/lib/10-way-to-build-and-preserve-better-boundaries#the-lowdown

Pomerance, M. (n.d.). *Why do boundaries make us feel bad?* The Candidly. https://www.thecandidly.com/2019/why-does-setting-boundaries-make-us-feel-like-terrible-people

Sheckles, L. (2016, May 9). *8 Ways setting boundaries improves your quality of life.* The Balanced Life. https://www.thebalancedlifellc.com/our-blog/123-individuals/374-8-ways-setting-boundaries-improves-your-quality-of-life

Silva Casabianca, S. (2022, October 28). *7 Signs someone doesn't respect your boundaries and what to do.* Psych Central. https://psychcentral.com/relationships/signs-boundary-violations#how-to-deal-with-boundary-violations

10 Types of boundary violations with betrayed partners and addicts. (n.d.). Trauma and Addiction Recovery Center. https://www.tarcrecovery.com/resources/10-types-of-boundary-violations-with-betrayed-partners-and-addicts

39 Inspirational Henry Cloud quotes (Boundaries). (2023, January 27). Gracious Quotes. https://graciousquotes.com/henry-cloud/

Tucker, M. (2021, May 14). *Part 11: Dealing with people who resist your boundaries.* Mad about Marriage. https://madaboutmarriage.com/2021/05/14/part-11-dealing-with-people-who-resist-your-boundaries/

TY. (2020, May 27). *7 Golden rules of relationships.* LinkedIn. https://www.linkedin.com/pulse/7-golden-rules-relationships-dominic-zenden/

What happens when our boundaries are crossed? (n.d.). Holistic Healing Counseling. https://holistichealingedmonton.com/blog/article/What+Happens+When+Our+Boundaries+Are+Crossed

/632#:~:text=A%20violation%20can%20happen%20when

When someone responds to your boundaries with anger. (2022, February 14). Boundaries Books. https://www.boundariesbooks.com/blogs/boundaries-blog/when-someone-responds-to-your-boundaries-with-anger

Whitener, S. (2019, December 11). *How setting boundaries positively impacts your self-esteem.* Forbes. https://www.forbes.com/sites/forbescoachescouncil/2019/12/11/how-setting-boundaries-positively-impacts-your-self-esteem/?sh=4229c1db339c

Why do people keep crossing your boundaries? (2016, July 16). The Overwhelmed Brain. https://theoverwhelmedbrain.com/crossing-your-boundaries/

Made in the USA
Coppell, TX
24 September 2023